# THE PUFFIN BOOK OF

## HOLIDAY STORIES

### INTRODUCTION BY
# RUSKIN BOND

### ILLUSTRATIONS BY
### RUJUTA THAKURDESAI

T0116581

PUFFIN BOOKS

An imprint of Penguin Random House

PUFFIN BOOKS

USA | Canada | UK | Ireland | Australia
New Zealand | India | South Africa | China

Puffin Books is part of the Penguin Random House group of companies
whose addresses can be found at global.penguinrandomhouse.com

Published by Penguin Random House India Pvt. Ltd
7th Floor, Infinity Tower C, DLF Cyber City,
Gurgaon 122 002, Haryana, India

Penguin
Random House
India

First published in Puffin Books by Penguin Random House India 2019

Text copyright © Penguin Books India 2019
Illustrations copyright © Rujuta Thakurdesai 2019

The copyright for the individual pieces vests with the respective authors.

A version of 'Crazy Uncle Ken' first appeared in *Crazy Times with Uncle Ken*
(2011); 'A Feast for Rats' in *The Land of Cards: Stories, Poems and Plays for
Children* (2010); and 'The Unending Story' in *Grandma's Bag of Stories* (2012),
all published by Penguin Books India.

10 9 8 7 6 5 4 3 2 1

ISBN 9780143447481

Typeset in Goudy Old Style by Manipal Digital Systems, Manipal
Printed at Thomson Press India Ltd, New Delhi

www.penguin.co.in

MIX
Paper
FSC FSC® C010615

# CONTENTS

# Contents

Contents

# INTRODUCTION

In India, not enough importance is given to writing for children. And what could be more important that the enrichment of young minds with great literature? This is when we discover ourselves, our own potential, and, more often than not, we'll do it through what we read and write.

Here are some of our best writers for children and young adults, and they have chosen to celebrate your holidays with stories *about* holidays. Of course, no two holidays are the same—for them or for the readers. And added to their varied experiences are a gem of a tale from Tagore as well as a little frivolity from my Uncle Ken.

Enjoy your holidays, dear readers. And wherever you go, don't forget to take a bag full of books with you. Holidays can become tedious without something to read.

*Ruskin Bond*

Ruskin Bond

It was the usual morning chaos in the Mehta household. Perhaps a little worse than usual, because there was a flight to be caught later that day, and, judging by the proceedings, it didn't look very likely that the Mehta family would be on it.

'But why do we have to go for two weeks? I'll miss Ayesha's birthday!' sulked thirteen-year-old Kiara as she hunted for her earphones, opening and shutting drawers with far more force than was necessary. 'She's the *only* friend I've made in this stuck-up new school. *And* she's having a pool party.'

Their father, Jai, who was currently sprawled across a suitcase, as if it were an opponent he had pinned down in a wrestling match, looked up from his rather unsuccessful attempts at shutting the bag.

'We'll have a pool *and* a beach at the hotel, Kiara,' he said between grunts. 'You can swim every day for the next two weeks if you like.'

'Hey, wait. Two weeks?' piped up Kiara's nine-year-old brother Aryan. 'But, Papa, you said we were only going for fifteen days. I don't want to miss the Liverpool-Chelsea game!'

Kiara rolled her eyes.

'And the Nobel Prize for maths is definitely going to my brother!' she muttered.

'But I want the Nobel Prize for football,' said Aryan, kicking an imaginary football into an imaginary goalpost and tearing around the room in a victory lap that caused a seismic shift in the fish tank and startled the goldfish into being even more goggle-eyed.

'Do we have to go by aeroplane? I don't like aeroplanes!' declared five-year-old Amaya, not willing to be left out of anything that her siblings were talking about.

'Do you know what is wrong with this generation?' panted Jai, who now looked like he was in the throes of the flying crow yoga pose, perched atop the suitcase in his ongoing struggle to shut it. 'There's absolutely no gratitude at all! When we were your age, the only place we went to for our holidays was to visit our Nanima-Nanabapa. Each and every holiday. And we were so happy doing that.'

Jai's mother, Pratibha, known to her family as Ba, took a loud slurp of her third cup of ginger tea and reluctantly shifted her attention from her riveting TV serial to her rather less enthralling family.

'*Why* is your foot stuck behind your elbow, Jai, and what are you muttering-puttering?' she asked. 'Don't tell me that you're still grumbling about having to visit my parents during your school vacations.'

'Whose side are you on, Ba?' wheezed Jai, while attempting to disentangle his foot from the crook of his elbow.

'How happy you sound about those holidays, Papa!' teased Kiara with a grin.

'We *were* happy!' said Jai, his foot now finally free to resume its normal duties. 'And what's more, our parents didn't have to spend every waking hour convincing us that where we were going was a good idea. We just got up and went wherever we were taken, without asking any questions.'

'Here we go again,' said Kiara under her breath. She spotted her earphones and let out a huge sigh of relief.

'But there were no Liverpool-Chelsea games then, Papa,' said Aryan.

'And you didn't have to go by aeroplane,' added Amaya.

'What's wrong with going by aeroplane, Amaya?' asked the children's mother, Kajal, who walked in, precariously balancing a mountain of foil-wrapped packets on her laptop bag.

'Have you forgotted, Ma? They tied us to the seats with those belts. And showed us those scary oskygen masks,' said Amaya, wide-eyed. 'And pointed to those doors from where we could run away—but they wouldn't open. Even the windows were stuck. I didn't like it at all.'

'You're so silly, Amaya,' said Aryan, clucking his tongue. 'If they open the windows and doors, all the food trays will fly out because they don't have seatbelts and then the pilot will starve, his eyes will get all blurry and he won't be able to see. And we'll crash!'

Aryan helpfully demonstrated this by diving headlong into the sofa, with sound effects to match.

Kiara turned to her parents with an exaggerated sigh.

'Are you sure these two are not adopted? Our family's collective IQ nosedives to staggering new lows with each passing day.'

'They're still little, Kiara. Don't be so unkind to your siblings,' said Kajal.

'Ah, there. We're done,' said Jai, casting an imperious glance at the suitcases he had finally managed to vanquish.

'But you forgot to put the theplas in, Jai!'

Jai looked at his wife in utter bewilderment.

'Are you serious, Kajal? It's not like we're headed to some desolate island where we have to hunt for food to avoid starvation. We're going to a resort that has a four-and-a-half star rating on TripAdvisor.'

'Yes, yes, but it's in Kerala, Jai. And you know me—I will begin to miss Gujarati food after two days.'

'Maybe we could just return as soon as Ma starts missing her home-cooked food?' interjected Kiara hopefully.

'Our trip is all paid for now . . .' began Jai.

'But, Papa, you told me that this trip was a prize given to Ma by her office for selling the most washing machines?' interrupted Aryan.

'Well, yes, we got a free trip for one week. But then we added on a second week, which we paid for, since we were going all the way and none of us had ever seen Kerala before.'

'I have,' said Amaya.

'I can't wait to hear about this,' mumbled Kiara.

Her mother shot her an admonishing look.

'A boy in my class brought Kerala in for show-and-tell,' continued Amaya. 'And we all got to pass it around. It was very prickly. And we made an alligator out of it in art class.'

'Er, Amaya, I think you're talking about a vegetable that sounds like Kerala,' said Kajal. 'This place we're going to is a beautiful part of south India. It's known as God's Own Country.'

'Okay, that's good,' said Amaya. 'I did secretly think it was silly to have a holiday with that prickly alligator thing. But I didn't want to hurt your feelings.'

Kajal wrapped her youngest in a bear hug.

'Promise me you'll always stay this way, my Amaya.'

'I know what you're doing, Ma,' huffed Kiara. 'You're trying to tell me that I don't think about anyone's feelings, right?'

'That is absolutely not true, Kia . . .' began Kajal.

'If you only like your children until they are five or nine or whatever age it is that I will never be again, then why don't you just send me away to boarding school!'

Kajal sighed. Talking to a teen was like navigating a minefield—one never knew what could blow up and when.

Meanwhile, Jai's single-minded focus on fitting the theplas into the suitcases had paid off.

'We did it!' he announced triumphantly, as if India had just won the World Cup.

'Oh, that's such a relief, Jai,' sighed Kajal.

'Who is going to feed my stick insects while we're away?' asked Aryan.

'Well, can't you just leave them a pile of leaves that they can keep eating?' suggested his mother.

'What! How would you like to be left a pile of stale theplas to eat, Ma?' countered Aryan, magnificently unimpressed by this preposterous suggestion. 'Also, I think one of them is going to lay eggs any day now, and I really wanted to film that.'

'It's great to see that you're taking so much interest in natural science,' said Jai approvingly, throwing a pointed look at Kiara.

'Oh, I'm just doing it to creep out this girl in my class who's terrified of insects,' Aryan said with a grin. 'I can't wait to see her expression when I show her the video. It's the only reason I've agreed to keep the stick insects at home over the holidays.'

'Ahem. Looks like Aryan's in the running for the Nobel Prize for science too, right, Papa?' snickered Kiara.

'Never mind him, Kiara. Why don't you go and get changed—those jeans are in tatters.'

'They're brand new, Papa!'

Ba harrumphed loudly. 'Tsk, unlike me, your father is behind the times, Kiara. I have already told the tailor that in your new shararas for Diwali, he should make holes in the knees, just like you have in your jeans.'

'Very funny, Ba,' said Kiara.

Ba ruffled Kiara's hair and turned her attention to her son.

'Jai, don't mind my saying this, but is it all right if I stay back?'

'What? Please, don't you start too now, Ba!'

'It's just that I don't understand why we are paying so much money to sleep in someone else's bed and use someone else's toilet, Jai.'

'It's a fancy hotel, Ba. We're not just landing up and taking over some random stranger's house,' said Jai, getting increasingly exasperated with his family.

'Well, I watched this programme on TV where there were secret cameras following the room service staff in this fancy hotel, and, do you know, they hardly clean anything at all. In fact,' Ba paused for effect, 'some of them lie on the beds and watch television!'

Ba's family looked suitably shocked, but one member suddenly seemed very animated.

'Yay!' cheered Aryan. 'So there will be a TV. I can watch the match on TV then.'

'And *that's* what you took away from Ba's story. Brilliant!' muttered Kiara.

'Ba, you can't believe everything you see on TV, you know,' said Jai. 'They make a lot of it up to improve viewer ratings and things.'

'Whatever you say, Jai. I just think there's nothing like being in one's own home.'

'What if we carry your sheets and towels, Ba?' offered Kajal.

'What? That's crazy!' sputtered Jai. 'Our suitcases are already stuffed to bursting. Where are all these sheets and towels going to fit?'

'I'm sure we can make some place, Jai,' said Kajal, patting his arm, 'if it will make Ba feel better about the trip.'

'So, we're carrying our own linen and our own food. Anything else you'd like to take? Beds?'

'Can we also take the cage with the stick insects?' asked Aryan.

'Sure,' said Jai, his voice dripping with sarcasm. 'Amaya? Would you like to add something to the list of things to take to God's Own Country?'

'But if that is God's country, whose country do we live in now?' asked Amaya.

Jai looked like his eyeballs would explode.

Kajal jumped into the conversation before it derailed completely, as things tended to do in their family.

'Amaya, let's talk more about this on the way to the airport. Does everyone have their bags packed and ready?'

'I need to get my sheets and towels,' announced Ba, heading purposefully to her room.

Jai shook his head in resignation.

'Don't worry so much, Jai. Picture the palm trees and the beaches,' said Kajal.

'All I'm picturing is hefty excess baggage charges.'

'It's going to be worth it,' said his wife. 'Come on, let's get going now!'

An hour and a half later, the Mehta family was in full force at the Mumbai airport.

'Did you take all our bags out of the taxi, Jai?' asked his mother.

'Yes, Ba, I did! And the bag with your sheets and towels is right here, under my nose.'

'I feel like I've forgotten something,' said Kajal. 'Oh, I need this break so badly!' She sighed loudly enough to make three passers-by look in her direction.

'You want to bet that she'll do her spin-cycle speech now?' whispered Kiara to Aryan.

'It's never-ending. Work. Home. Kids. Cooking. Homework. Repeat. It's like I'm on the spin cycle of a washing machine. Non-stop!' said Kajal.

'Told you,' said Kiara smugly.

'Huh?' said Aryan, far more interested in the aroma of samosas wafting his way than in his sister's endless commentary.

'You can hang out to dry in Kerala, Kajal,' teased Jai, giving her a hug.

'When people pee in an aeroplane, is that why it rains?' asked Amaya.

'Yes, that's exactly right, Amaya,' said Kiara with a straight face. 'Did you work that out all by yourself?'

'Yes,' said Amaya, very chuffed to have impressed her big sister. 'But what happens if they need to poo?'

'Well,' said Kiara. 'That's when we get snow. The poo gets smaller and loses its smell and colour as it falls through the atmosphere. And some people catch snowflakes on their tongues. Imagine that.'

'Ewww!' said Amaya in shock and awe.

'Maybe you can do a show-and-tell about it,' said Kiara, plugging in her earphones to prevent any further conversation. She had a sneaking feeling she'd reached her daily limit of wickedness.

'Let's head to the check-in counter,' said Jai. 'Where is Aryan? One blink and that boy disappears!'

'Not again!' said Kajal, her panic rising by the second, as her eyes scanned the heaving throng for signs of Aryan. 'You search that side, Jai, I'll look this side.'

'Airports are notorious for disappearances,' pronounced Ba gravely, keeping a protective hand on her suitcase in case it too went missing like the grandson.

Twenty agonizing minutes later, Kajal finally spotted Aryan, with his face glued to the samosa counter. She managed to reel him in, using a packet of samosas as bait, to join the rest of the family.

'You'd better eat these quickly,' she said. 'They don't allow any food through security check.'

'Aryan has a trick where he can store food in his back like a camel,' said Amaya. 'Show them, Aryan.'

'Er, let's save that for later. Let's just get in the check-in queue now,' said Jai.

'Did you remember to put ribbons on our suitcases, Jai?' asked Ba. 'I watched this programme on TV where these drug dealers exchanged suitcases with a normal family like ours. And then that family spent ten years in jail.'

'*When* are you watching all these programmes, Ba?' asked Jai.

'But, Ba, how do the ribbons keep drug dealers away?' asked Aryan in muffle-speak, through a mouthful of samosa.

'It's obvious, Aryan,' chimed in Kiara. 'If you're a drug dealer, it's not cool to walk around with suitcases that have ribbons. No one will take you seriously.'

Aryan nodded, seeing the obvious sense in this.

'Don't worry, Ba, our suitcases have ribbons on them,' said Kajal.

'Did anyone check the weather in Madras?' asked Ba.

'We're going to Kerala, Ba. Everything in south India is not Madras,' said Jai. 'And Madras is now called Chennai, by the way.'

'Pah! It's all very confusing,' grumbled Ba. 'They keep changing the names of everything. Even this airport. While they were at it, they could have added some more words to the name Chhatrapati Shivaji Maharaj International Airport Mumbai, no?'

'Ba, you should have your own stand-up comedy show,' chuckled Kiara.

'Hmm. Good idea. Aryan, will you record me when we're back? Then we could put it on ViewTube?'

'You mean YouTube? Sure, Ba, but I need to record my stick insects laying eggs first, if that's okay?'

'No problem,' said Ba. 'I can start by practising on these bored passengers in this queue.'

'Which, incidentally, doesn't seem to be moving at all. Should we just go home, Ma?'

'Don't be silly, Kiara. Perhaps I should go to the top of the line and tell them we have a flight that is about to leave?'

'Everyone here has a flight that is about to leave, Ma! They're not just hanging out in this queue with packed suitcases for fun.'

Just then, a metallic voice sounded through the loudspeakers. 'This is the last and final boarding call for Jet Airways flight 9W 2403 to Kochi.'

'Er . . . right. Let's maybe go with your "top of the line" plan, Ma,' mumbled Kiara sheepishly.

After five minutes of much jostling and justifying, the Mehta family finally reached the Jet Airways check-in counter. Kajal handed over the tickets to the airline official, who punched some keys on his computer and then squinted at the screen, adjusting his spectacles.

'Sorry, could you please hurry? Our flight is to leave shortly,' said Jai, pointing to his wrist even though it didn't have a watch on it.

The official peered at the Mehtas from over his spectacles.

'I'm sorry, but these tickets have been cancelled,' he said.

'What!' exclaimed Kajal.

'What!' echoed the rest of the Mehtas.

'Show them your Omega India Salesperson of the Year certificate, Kajal,' said Jai. 'There must be some mistake.'

Kajal rifled around in her handbag for the certificate and happened to spot her phone instead. Someone was calling her. In fact, someone had called her twenty-three times.

'It's my boss calling. This will sort things out,' said Kajal to the perplexed airline official as she answered the phone. 'Hello?'

Her family leaned in to listen.

'Oh! Er, sorry about the twenty-three missed calls, Mr Taneja. My phone was on silent. There's been a lot going on. But I'm so glad you've called. There seems to be some confusion about the tickets.'

Kajal's expression changed as she listened to what Mr Taneja had to say.

'I see. Well, I guess I'd like to hear the bad news first, Mr Taneja,' said Kajal, most flustered by the proceedings.

She listened, nodding at intervals and looking crestfallen and indignant in turn.

'Mix-up?' she finally spluttered. 'But *how* could there have been a mix-up, Mr Taneja?'

'Ba was right. The drug dealers have mixed up our bags and tricked us,' declared Aryan conspiratorially.

'Show this airline man the ribbons on our suitcases. Then they'll know we're not drug dealers.'

'Will we all be in jail now because of the drugs?' asked Amaya.

'Shhh, you two,' whispered Ba, casting furtive glances all around.

The passengers behind them exchanged strange looks.

'So does this mix-up in the sales figures mean that our trip is cancelled, Mr Taneja?' continued Kajal.

'Breaking news! It's not a mix-up of suitcases—it's washing machines,' announced Kiara. 'They've miscounted the washing machines that Ma had sold. Their maths seems as good as yours, Aryan.'

Aryan was busy spotting possible drug dealers, blissfully oblivious to his sister's comments. Just as the rest of the Mehtas were blissfully oblivious to the boiling wake of airport rage that their bottleneck was creating.

'Could you all please step out of the queue?' snapped the airline official, wishing he had taken the day off instead of having to deal with this spectacularly flaky family and the swelling crescendo of disgruntled passengers.

'We can still go, Kajal. We have our own week booked,' said Jai, one foot still in the queue.

'But that's next week, Jai. And we'll need to book new flight tickets,' said Kajal, cupping her hand over the phone.

'What about the good news? Ask that Juneja-Buneja!' Ba prompted hoarsely from behind, loud enough for Mr Taneja to hear.

As Kajal listened to Mr Taneja's 'good news', her eyes widened.

'What! Worldwide?' she exclaimed, quite overcome.

'There's a worldwide search for us now,' said Aryan. 'We're wanted by the police of every country.'

'In which country's jail will we live?' asked Amaya.

'Thank you so much, Mr Taneja,' gushed Kajal before she hung up.

'Why is she thanking him? Grown-ups are so weird,' muttered Kiara.

Kajal looked around at her family.

'So our Kerala trip is cancelled . . .' she began.

'Did the drug dealers switch our bags, Ma?'

'Aryan! Can I *please* finish?' said Kajal, sighing in exasperation. 'It's cancelled because when they rechecked the sales figures, they found that I was the Omega *Worldwide* Salesperson of the Year! So we've won a two-week trip to Europe instead!'

'What? That's phenomenal, Kajal!' exclaimed Jai.

'This is just like that reality TV show I had watched,' said Ba.

'That's huge, Ma,' said Kiara.

'That's almost as cool as being a drug dealer,' conceded Aryan.

'Are we going to jail?' asked Amaya.

'I'm telling Ayesha I can attend her party!' said Kiara, pulling out her phone.

'Let's head back home,' said Jai. 'And maybe now we can plan a three-week holiday in Europe.'

There was pin-drop silence. Which lasted five seconds.

'Hey, wait. First you said fifteen days. Then you made it two weeks. How has it become three weeks now?' questioned Aryan.

'I don't want to be stuck with these two photobombing my life for three weeks!' said Kiara.

'I don't want to go on an aeroplane,' said Amaya.

Kajal Mehta took a long, deep breath. 'I think I might cancel my leave and get back to work. I *really* do need a break!' she said.

Another five-second silence followed. Which was broken by a chorus of young Mehtas in discordant unison.

'But I've already posted on Snapchat that we're going to Europe!' moaned Kiara.

'Europe sounds cool. Isn't Liverpool the capital of Europe?' pondered Aryan.

'Are we still going to jail?' asked Amaya hopefully.

'Look, look, it's taking off,' said Ba. 'That must be the flight to Madras that we just missed.'

And much like the Mehta family's plans, within seconds, the Jet Airways flight to Kochi was up in the air.

# A RUINED HOLIDAY

Paro Anand

It was official. My holidays were RUINED.

It wasn't like I was being dramatic or anything. I knew that it was no one's fault. Least of all my grandmother's. Of course she didn't fall on purpose. I *knew* that. I mean, who would fall and break a hip on purpose? I wasn't being mean, you know. But it just wasn't fair that she fell on the last day of school. Just as my parents were getting ready to come for the play in which I had finally, finally got a major role. And it was going to be one of those rare occasions when Dad was going to be coming too. I'm one of those students whose dad is never there for PTA meetings or sports days and stuff. Not that I would want him there on sports day, when the only thing I usually participate in is the tug of war. I'm always the anchor. You know, the fattest one who literally has to throw their weight around. But the play was a different thing. I really, really wanted him to come and see me turn into the corrupt minister who makes everyone's life miserable by . . . you guessed it, throwing his weight around.

But Nani fell in the bathroom and shouted out as loud as she could. Mum and Dad found her on the floor, hip broken and unable to get up. I didn't know any of it. I was dressed and ready in my kurta-pyjama and drawn-on moustache, scanning the audience for a familiar face while delivering my lines. I knew I missed a few. I knew that I didn't do as well as I had in rehearsals. Because half of me was wondering where Mum and Dad were.

I know what you're thinking. What an insensitive person! But that's not true. I'm a sensitive kind of guy. It's just that I was disappointed. And then, when I got home to fight with them about it, I couldn't even do that because Mum was in tears and Dad was on the phone informing everyone that there was going to be a surgery the next day. A hip replacement. Which sounded kind of cool but also scary.

So, instead of fighting with anyone, I made myself a sandwich and generally felt sad. Sad for my grandma too, by the way, just in case you were thinking I'm selfish too.

Nani's operation went well, and she was soon home . . . which was great. I mean, mostly. The thing is, she was supposed to have gone to my masi's house for the summer vacation, and we were meant to go to Russia. I'd really been looking forward to it too. I'd read about all the things you could do there. I especially wanted to see the embalmed body of Lenin . . . or was it Stalin? Keep getting the two of them mixed up. Besides, there was so much to do. And we were to go to St Petersburg, where the summer solstice is celebrated and it's never night. Like, it never gets dark at all. It's called the White Nights.

Instead, Nani came back home from hospital because, of course, she couldn't travel now. And so we couldn't travel either. I tried to be brave and hide my disappointment and said, 'No, no, of course not' when Mum asked if I was sad about the trip being called off. But of course I was. I mean, you get it, right?

But things got even worse. Mum and Dad decided that since we were not going, they were going to cancel their leave and go back to work. Which made sense, except that they decided to leave me in charge. I was just ten years old! How could they have forgotten that small fact? I was a child, I protested. But they were soon out the door, leaving me to keep Nani company, along with the nurse and our cook.

I like Nani, I do, but . . . but is that really how you'd want to spend your holiday? You tell me. My other friends at school were going on all kinds of dope holidays. Cruises and hikes and stuff. And there I was, playing nurse to poor Nani. Poor me too. And I couldn't even say anything to anyone, because then I'd be thought of as selfish. Which I'm not. Really.

And as though that wasn't girly enough, there was something else that was happening in our family. Or rather, was about to happen. My aunt, my masi, was going to have a baby. I knew they had been wanting a baby for a while. And in a couple of months there was one coming. I was as excited about it as a normal ten-year-old could be expected to be. Which wasn't very.

The holidays dragged on. Nani was trying not to be too demanding. Which was sweet of her, and I really appreciated it. But I was bored stupid.

Then one morning, Nani asked me to pull out a big cardboard carton that she had tucked away in the corner of her room and empty its contents on her bed. I'd expected something exciting, something precious. Something. What I didn't expect was a DISASTER. A disaster of old, shabby clothes, some not even whole clothes but bits and pieces of clothes.

Nani saw my look, my turned-up nose, and she laughed.

'Yes,' she giggled. 'I am a batty old lady, aren't I? I agree with you wholeheartedly.'

'No, no . . .' I stammered, 'that's not what I . . .' But, of course, she had read my face perfectly. She knew what I had thought.

'Well, in my day, we didn't waste anything. We kept it all away and made use of every little bit of everything we had. Because we didn't have much to begin with, so we had to make it all last as long as possible.'

'But what's the use of all these?' I said, picking up one strip of flowery material. 'What could you possibly do with it?'

'All right, I agree. What could you do with an old, old dress like that? But close your eyes for a minute.

28

Hold the cloth against your cheek. Feel how soft it is. Like the finest silk in the world.'

I did it. And yes, the cloth was soft. No doubt about it. But so what?

'And now let this bit of cloth slip through your fingers. Close your eyes, and it will feel like the coolest butter running through your fingers.'

Okay . . . I've never had cool butter running through my fingers, but I guess that's what it would feel like.

Before we go any further, let me tell you that my nani had been more of a forbidding grandmother, and to her I was just a noisy child. I don't know how a broken hip made so much difference, but she suddenly started to talk to me as though I were an adult. Like really, really talk to me. Like I was her favourite child. She began to tell me stories. They poured out of her as though the broken hip had broken a seal on them.

'What I'm going to do with these bits and pieces of clothes is make the softest little quilt for the softest little baby that's on its way.'

'From old clothes?' I couldn't keep the surprise and disgust from my voice. I mean, *chhee*, the thought of a newborn baby wrapped up in old clothes wasn't pleasant. It's not as if we were that desperately poor or something.

'These are not just old clothes. Each of these pieces of cloth has been bought and worn with love and joy. Each of them carries a memory and a blessing from the original wearer to the new baby.'

I continued to look puzzled. She thought for a moment, then reached for a tiny indigo shirt.

'This is the first garment ever worn by your nana. The day your grandfather was born, he was put into this. And this very shirt was part of his father's school uniform; he wore it on his first day so many, many years ago. So, you see, this piece that you see as a torn old garment carries the blessings of long life and good education from two separate generations.'

I took the piece of cloth from her and held it against my cheek. It whispered softly into my ear, telling me secrets. I chucked it back down immediately. I was going soft in the head, thinking these thoughts. I mean, really. But then my eye fell on another really nice fabric.

'And this one?' I asked, picking up a flowered, patterned little dress.

'Ah, this one. This was first worn by your mother on her first birthday. Then when your masi turned one, we fell on very hard times. Your grandfather was very ill, and we had to close down our business and spend almost every last rupee on his treatment. I couldn't afford a luxury like a new dress. And I washed and pressed this one and put your masi in it. Didn't she look like a royal princess in it . . .'

'How are you going to turn all this into a quilt?'

'We call this a *guddri*, which really means something to cuddle into. You fold the cloth over and over, and then you make a pattern of squares with other pieces of cloth and stitch them together, using the folded bits as fillers and the squares as the cover.

'In the old days, babies were always wrapped up in a guddri. Now, of course, most people buy one. But since I am sitting about all day, I decided to try my hand at making one again.'

I watched as she began to draw the clothes out one by one, laying them out on the bed in front of her, smoothening the creases with her gnarled old fingers. But there was love in those hands, a smile on her face that made me want to watch for a little while. Yes, I felt a little silly. But it was like watching someone put together a cloth jigsaw puzzle.

She didn't say anything, just looked up as though seeing me for the first time, standing there. And then she patted her bed, inviting me to join her.

*Okay*, I told myself, *just for a little while.*

Each little cloth had a story of its own. The parts of the cloth that were whole were cut into squares. The parts that were a bit torn and frayed were folded into little feather-soft bundles.

'What's this one?' I asked, picking up an old white shirt, soft with age.

'This is the shirt that your grandfather wore to court when he fought his first case as a new lawyer. Didn't he look handsome. He was so tall that I had to get a stool to stand on to do the *aarti* and put tilak to wish him good luck as he went off.'

The first day of quilting was over too soon. Nani got tired easily and needed to lie down. But I was waiting to get back to it, hear more stories. I started to feel that when she picked up a cloth, started to tell its story, those long-ago moments came alive again. Almost as if I were watching a movie about my family. I started recognizing a particular gleam in her eyes when there was a story coming. I'd settle in with her and, sure enough, there was another little family treasure or secret to savour.

There was a beautiful sari that was part of my grandmother's trousseau, my mother's first uniform when she started school, my great-aunt's silk shirt that her husband presented to her when they got married, my great-grandfather's nightshirt, which we laughed about because it looked like a nightie for women. It was as if they were all sitting with us, day after day, laughing with us, telling us their stories. I learnt so much about my family.

When it came time to stitch it all together, Nani found that she couldn't thread the needle. So I started doing that for her. From there it was only a short step—I shared the job of stitching too. I loved it. It wasn't easy, but I loved it.

'I hope no one ever sees me doing this, Nani,' I giggled.

'Why?'

'I mean, my friends. I'd be the butt of all jokes.'

'But why?'

'A boy spending his vacation stitching for a little baby. Of course they'd laugh at me.'

I saw that look in her eye and knew there was a story or something coming.

'When I was a little girl, I wanted to ride our horse.'

'Our horse? You had a horse? I thought you were poor.'

'Oh, we weren't poor, just that we fell on hard times for a while. And yes, we had a horse, many people did then. Because we didn't have cars.'

That was a shock. I didn't know anyone who didn't have a car. I mean, no one among my family and friends. But I kept quiet.

She continued, 'So I wanted to ride a horse, but girls were not supposed to. My father learnt of it when I fell off the horse and hurt my knee. As soon as he got to know, he bought me a pair of breeches and a shirt and taught me to ride. Yes, there were people who were upset, people who thought it wasn't right. A girl in trousers was a big no-no. A girl riding around on a horse was absolutely unheard of. But my father said, "The day society dictates what my children can do is the day I have failed them." And so I rode horses, I went to university in a city far from home. No one could put me in a box. My advice to you is to never be afraid to do what you love. If you feel like sewing, if you feel like making a guddri for your little cousin, don't let anyone make fun of you for it. There is no law that says boys cannot learn to sew a button or knit a sweater.'

'Knit a sweater? I couldn't do that!' I protested, still giggling at the image of me knitting.

Little did I know that I would soon knit myself a sweater. Not all of it, of course. My grandmother helped. It took me a whole year. Almost up to the next summer vacation. But it was wonderful, and I loved it.

Meanwhile, the baby's quilt was almost complete. And Nani had started to take short walks in the park too. I would walk with her sometimes. I even bumped into some of my classmates, who may or may not have sniggered to see me walking with my grandmother. But I didn't care. I loved being with her. She was the best company.

And then the day came when we were ready to add the final stitches to the baby's blanket. Nani suggested that we put in a special message for the baby.

Nani wrote her message in Punjabi. '*Rab rakha*,' she read to me. It meant 'may God be always by your side'.

On to a fragment of my great-grandfather's shirt, I wrote with a marker, 'Never be afraid to do what you love.'

And then it was done. The final stitch was in.

The ruined holiday had turned out to be the most perfect holiday after all.

# SWALLOWED BY A SNAKE

Jane De Suza

How could I have been swallowed by a snake and still be telling you this story?

Well, you'll have to wait, won't you? Kids nowadays have no patience, no, none at all. As much patience as a snake has knees.

I'll have you know that I'm eighty years old, not dead yet, thank you very much.

No, this isn't a ghost story about . . . You know what, no more questions till the story starts.

In my boyhood, trains hauled by coal engines chugged across the country. We waited endlessly for the summer holidays to make that dusty trip from Kalimpong to Goa, changing trains over three days and emerging like sacks of coal ourselves.

On the way back, my mother would stuff every bit of her own childhood memories into gunny bags to carry back. Red chillies, which, if the bags burst, would keep us coughing in contest with the puffing engine; vinegar because she claimed there was nothing as pure as Goan vinegar, till two bottles cracked and every kid claimed every other one had wet the bunk; and once she even got back those tiny dried fish that let out such a massive stink that the ticket collector threatened to throw us out, along with our bags, at the next stop.

Ah, alright, I must really start at the beginning, not the end of the trip, you're right.

Goa was like a jungle to us. My grandmother's house was surrounded by trees growing wild, shedding every kind of fruit—mangoes, cashews, guavas and especially coconuts—onto the high-tiled roof in the middle of stormy nights. 'That's the ghost of the Ghats trying to enter,' Fabio would whisper under our mosquito nets.

Yes, yes, I did tell you this wasn't a ghost story, so don't run away yet.

Fabio was my slightly older cousin who lived in Goa and was the target of our envy for this reason alone. We imagined him swinging through trees all day, while we hunched over incomprehensible 'Fill in the blanks' in classrooms where the masters had canes and would gleefully use them.

While on holiday, we spent all day in the sun, of course, up on those trees, swinging, climbing, chasing each other, or exploring the wilderness beyond, right up to the creek. Going outdoors was an adventure on its own. We encountered enough species to start our own zoo.

During a game of hide-and-seek one morning, I was crouched in some dense shrubbery, hiding from Rosa, another of my numerous cousins, whose school-teacherly sing-song voice grew nearer. 'I can see you, Rinaldo,' she fibbed. I had to shove my finger between my teeth to stop from giggling. As the suspense grew, something heavy brushed against me. I stumbled and bit the finger I'd stuffed into my mouth. It was a pig. And another. A squealing throng of pigs and piglets was running through the shrubs. Naturally, I squealed even louder. And Rosa pounced on me.

Pigs running amok; hens, chickens and roosters squawking in alarm and getting underfoot; monkeys doing their trapeze act; the many dogs and cats that my grandma fed sunning themselves on the wooden balcony seats; cows chewing cud, dolefully eyeing me when I got too close; and one bad-tempered bull with awful eyesight just charging at anything it felt like, even a swaying branch.

Will you stop asking me that? I'm coming to the snake. You've got to understand how we all lived then; animals and birds too—screeching parrots, crows, hawks and sparrows—were just part of the family. They ate up all the leftovers and kept our back garden clean.

There were rats as big as cats and mongooses as big as dogs. Because, you see, anywhere there are snakes, there are mongooses. And there were snakes all over, outdoors and sometimes indoors too. You'd open a door to the courtyard in your pyjamas, eyes still clouded with sleep, and something would plop on to your shoulder and slither away before you had even exited your last dream.

My grandma wouldn't let us harm the snakes. They kept away the rats, she said. And most of them were less harmful than we kids were. The snakes didn't break windows or elbows or priceless porcelain vases passed down from grandfathers. They slithered harmlessly on their way.

'You know we have a pet snake?' whispered Fabio one evening as dusk set its purple cape over the house.

'What?' I glanced around nervously. 'I haven't seen one in a while.'

'You'd better not. If you see it, you're dead.' Fabio squinted dramatically. 'It's a killer pet. Its name is Demonio, and it has green slits for eyes that can hypnotize you. It's six feet long and as thick as my thigh, and its tongue is the length of my arm.'

I gulped, the demon snake slithering out from my imagination and into reality so well that I could almost see it behind Fabio now. 'And its poison,' Fabio continued, eyes lit up like coal embers. 'It shoots poison out across the entire garden, so it can kill anyone—*thop*! Just like that.' Fabio collapsed sideways, his eyes rolling back and his tongue lolling out, flipping and flopping like a fish out of water.

My aunt happened to walk in right then with her candle, which she brought out at dusk to light the lanterns around the house. She almost tripped over the poisoned Fabio writhing on the floor. Annoyed, she gave her son a tiny kick with her foot.

'I'm dying of a snakebite,' he protested.

'Die later. Get up; go get some coconut fibre to keep the stove burning.'

The fibre acquired, we were all put to other chores in the setting up of dinner. There were twenty-three of us that summer. Nine adults and fourteen children from all branches of the family, including two cousins we didn't even know dangled from our family tree.

Fabio had been separated from me and was made to sit at the other end of the long table, on a stool from which only the top of his spiky hair could be seen. My normally hearty appetite was somewhat tempered by my imagination. I could only see those green slits of eyes in the pea and coconut curry.

After dinner, I helped my mother and her sister, my aunt, draw water from the well to pour into the fat earthenware pots.

'Rinaldo!' My mother knocked her knuckles on my head, a little too hard for comfort. 'Concentrate on what you're doing. You're slopping water all over the place and making the ground all slippery. We'll fall into the well if we slip.'

My aunt cackled loudly. 'And we wouldn't want that, no? What with that snake living in the well.'

'The snake,' I gasped. 'It lives in the well? Why do you have a snake in the well?'

My aunt kept laughing. 'It eats up the frogs and insects that fall in. It keeps our water clean. That's our pet snake.'

Demonio! I paled.

My aunt and my mother had turned back, carrying the pots towards the kitchen, instructing me to continue drawing water. Shivering even in that Goa heat, I leaned over the wall of the well to throw the pail back in.

That's when I saw it.

The green eyes glaring up at me, the long tongue leaping out while the massive black snake uncoiled from the depths of the well and struck out, its poison arcing up like lightning. I grabbed the thing nearest me, the tall ceramic statue of St Anthony of Padua, the Goans' most loved saint. With every last ounce of muscle power, I heaved it at the demon snake, toppling over myself.

The splash carried across the darkness.

My mother screamed, and my aunt began to yell towards the house at the menfolk and the children. 'Come here, you fools, hurry up.'

Both women dropped their pots and ran wildly back towards the well. I wasn't where they'd left me. The men had rushed over too, with children scrambling between legs, trying for a look.

'Rinaldo's fallen into the well,' my aunt wailed.

'Go get him.' My mother began to beat on my father's back. 'Go, go!'

'But I can't swim,' my city-bred father protested.

'It's okay,' my uncle said. 'Lots of people fall into wells here. Our wells aren't dangerous.'

'Except for the snake,' Fabio cried.

That was the first time my mother collapsed.

'Throw some water on her,' someone suggested.

'Don't be a fool,' my aunt barked. 'If you throw the pail into the well, it will hit poor Rinaldo's head.'

'Rinaldo! Rinaldooooooo!' my two sisters screamed into the depths of the well, their voices echoing back to them from its secretive depths. 'We won't lock you up in the bathroom again. Come out.'

'You did what?' My aunt slapped the one closest to her.

In the panic and the screaming, the neighbours, though the farthest was half a kilometre away, all came over, lanterns dancing, advice flowing freely.

Joachim, my only cousin who could boast a cycle of his own, was sent to call Doctor Rozario, and Fabio was sent to call Joao, the leading lad who jumped into wells in the name of tradition during the feast of St Joao (his actual name had long since been buried in official records since he'd earned this title).

'Rinaldooooooo!' The screams kept echoing into the well.

The women started the rosary, fingers fumbling over beads, eyes darting towards the well for the miracle that the rosary no doubt would bring about.

Joao arrived and peeled off his clothes in a splendid display of sportsmanship, and, with a loud prayer, he jumped into the well, just like that. *Thop*, as Fabio would have said.

Dr Rozario, who had been pulled out of his nephew's engagement dinner, was rather less enthusiastic, but waited nonetheless.

After a short while, Joao's voice floated up from deep down. 'He is not here, swimming or floating.'

My mother collapsed a second time.

'Look well. Dive deep,' my father implored.

After a little while longer, Joao tugged on the rope. 'Pull me up. I cannot find the boy here.'

He was pulled up, and he bent over, gasping. 'I will have to call my friends. He may be at the bottom.'

Dr Rozario left for his dinner party. There was nothing he could do with no patient, was there?

There was more wailing and beating of hands against heads; the prayers rose in pitch.

My grandma then sent Joachim to call Father Anton.

'Why a priest?' asked my sister.

'You know, just in case,' my uncle hemmed and hawed.

In case. In case I had bumped my head and died. In case I had drowned. In case I had been swallowed by a snake.

Fabio, meanwhile, had been howling so loudly that many aunts had thumped him. 'Keep quiet!'

'He's been swallowed by the snake.' Fabio clutched his throat dramatically. 'By Demonio.'

My mother, who had just been resuscitated, fainted again. Fabio was thumped a few more times, told to shut up and get it together, and go call Dr Rozario again, to tend to my mother this time.

Now, here's a secret.

Wait, wait, I'm getting to it. An old man needs to stop for a sip of water, at least. You needn't jump all over me. Or I'll change this story to 'Swallowed by My Grandkids' instead of 'Swallowed by a Snake'.

So, the secret.

I wasn't even in the well.

When I realized that I'd thrown the sacred statue of our beloved St Anthony into the well, and the splash announced my evil-doing, I flew into a panic. I knew I'd be in everyone's bad books for the rest of the holiday—the rest of my life—to put it mildly.

Naturally, I wasn't brave enough to dive into the well and rescue St Anthony from the snake. After all, we were talking about Demonio here. He of the crippling poison and the coiled, muscled body. No, no, no.

It was a split-second decision taken in the time it took my aunt and my mother to drop their pots and turn around. Luckily, it was so dark in the garden, with the overhanging branches of the trees and the general murkiness, that they couldn't see the well from where they stood. Or me.

I scooted.

By the time my worrying family had gathered around the well, I was up in the branches of the closest mango tree. Hidden in its abundance of leaves, I peered down.

Huddled out of sight, I had a decent view of the panic I'd created, with no idea how to ingratiate myself back into the picture. A walloping for sure. In my feverish state of mind, I made plans to go catch the train back home, bus back to some other town, boat back to some other shore . . . I'd start over, work instead of go to school, make millions, buy many more statues of every saint my grandma held close. Illogically and frantically, I built taller stories of escape to richness and fame, a small voice inside protesting at leaving my parents and two annoying sisters.

Meanwhile, the village's young lads were taking turns jumping into the well, but with no luck. No one found even a hair off my head. It's a saying, a saying.

My grandma suddenly threw up her hands and began to loudly invoke the powers of St Anthony. The saint was approached for all sorts of lost things, which miraculously turned up soon enough: bags, money, shoes, dogs, needles—and little boys.

The cluster of people turned towards the statue of St Anthony to cajole him into returning me to the land of the living, when they noticed he wasn't standing there at all.

The wails that went up were even louder. The snake of the well was now not satisfied with frogs and rats—it had demanded a little boy and now a saint.

At that very moment, one of the well-divers came up for air, triumphantly holding up a large piece of the plaster that the statue was made of. 'St Anthony!' my grandma cried. 'He dived into the well to save our boy.'

There was a fresh round of tears.

It was almost two in the morning when the exhausted divers finally gave up. The police, of course, were far from anyone's mind. What would they do? Dive? Pray? Ask questions?

My mother was carried into the house after Dr Rozario gave her a heavier-than-needed dose of something that knocked her straight out. It was decided that the search and dive would begin at the crack of dawn, when they could see clearer.

As luck would have it, I didn't last till dawn. Not very used to falling asleep in trees, I quite obviously flipped over in my sleep and tumbled right out.

The second crash of the night brought everyone panicking again, holding lanterns and candles and rosaries and stout sticks.

It was fleet-footed Fabio who found me lying on the ground. Every bone in my body ached, but it was my ears he almost punctured with his excited shout. 'Rinaldo! He's alive. The snake spat him out.'

I was about to tell him what had really happened, but the crowd gathered me up in their arms, crying and praying over me, patting my head, kissing my hands. And so, I decided to keep quiet—wouldn't you have?

Anyway, I was fed well and made much of. Everyone was delighted to see me, except, of course, poor Dr Rozario, who was pulled out of bed a couple of hours after he'd finally slipped in.

I later hopped over to the well before I left Goa and winked into its inky darkness. 'Thanks, Demonio, you made me a hero.'

My grandma started every party with the proud introduction of her brood of grandkids. 'This is Rosa, who plays the violin. This is Joachim, who is studying to be a doctor . . .' Down the ranks till she would pull me at last into her arms.

'And this is Rinaldo, who was swallowed by a snake.'

CRAZY UNCLE KEN

Ruskin Bond

Every winter, when I came home from boarding school, I would spend about a month with Granny, before going on to spend the rest of the holidays with my mother and stepfather. My parents couldn't cook.

They employed a khansama—a professional cook— who made a good mutton curry but little else. Mutton curry for lunch and mutton curry for dinner can be a bit tiring, especially for a boy who liked to eat almost everything.

Granny was glad to have me because she lived alone most of the time. Not entirely alone, though . . . There was a gardener, Dhuki, who lived in an outhouse. And he had a son called Mohan, who was about my age. And there was Ayah, an elderly maidservant who helped with the household work. And there was a Siamese cat with bright blue eyes and a mongrel dog called Crazy, because he ran circles round the house.

And, of course, there was Uncle Ken, Granny's only son, who came to stay whenever he was out of a job (which was quite often) or when he felt like enjoying some of Granny's cooking.

So Granny wasn't really alone. All the same, she was glad to have me. She didn't enjoy cooking for herself, she said; she had to cook for *someone*. And although the cat and the dog, and sometimes Uncle Ken, appreciated her efforts, a good cook likes to have a boy to feed, because boys are adventurous and ready to try the most unusual dishes.

Whenever Granny tried out a new recipe on me, she would wait for my comments and reactions, and then make a note in one of her exercise books. These notes were useful when she made the dish again, or when she tried it out on others.

'Do you like it?' she'd ask after I'd taken a few mouthfuls.

'Yes, Gran.'

'Sweet enough?'

'Yes, Gran.'

'Not *too* sweet?'

'No, Gran.'

'Would you like some more?'

'Yes, please, Gran.'

'Well, finish it off.'

'If you say so, Gran.'

Roast duck. This was one of Granny's specials. The first time I had roast duck at Granny's place, Uncle Ken was there too.

He'd just lost a job as a railway guard and had come to stay with Granny until he could find another job. He always stayed as long as he could, only moving on when Granny offered to get him a job as an assistant master in Padre Lal's Academy for Small Boys. Uncle Ken couldn't stand small boys. They made him nervous, he said. I made him nervous too, but there was only one of me, and there was always Granny to protect him. At Padre Lal's, there were over a hundred small boys.

Although Uncle Ken had a tremendous appetite and ate just as much as I did, he never praised Granny's dishes. I think this is why I was annoyed with him at times, and why, sometimes, I enjoyed making him feel nervous.

Uncle Ken looked down at the roast duck, his glasses slipping down to the edge of his nose.

'Hmm . . . Duck again?'

'What do you mean, duck again? You haven't had duck since you were here last month,' retorted Granny.

'That's what I mean,' said Uncle Ken. 'Somehow, one expects more variety from you.'

All the same, he took two large helpings and ate most of the stuffing before I could get at it. I took my revenge by emptying all the apple sauce on to my plate.

Uncle Ken knew I loved the stuffing, and I knew he was crazy about Granny's apple sauce. So we were even.

'When are you joining your parents?' he asked hopefully, over the jam tart.

'I may not go to them this year,' I said. 'When are you getting another job, Uncle?'

'Oh, I'm thinking of taking rest for a couple of months.'

I enjoyed helping Granny and Ayah with the washing up. While we were at work, Uncle Ken would take a siesta on the veranda or switch on the radio to listen to dance music. Glenn Miller and his swing band were all the rage then.

'And how do you like your Uncle Ken?' asked Granny one day, as she emptied the bones from his plate into the dog's bowl.

'I wish he was someone else's uncle,' I said.

'He's not so bad, really. Just eccentric.'

'What's eccentric?'

'Oh, just a little crazy.'

'At least Crazy runs round the house,' I said. 'I've never seen Uncle Ken running.'

But I did one day.

Mohan and I were playing marbles in the shade of the mango grove when we were taken aback by the sight of Uncle Ken charging across the compound, pursued by a swarm of bees. He'd been smoking a cigar under a silk-cotton tree, and the fumes had disturbed the wild bees in their hive, directly above him. Uncle Ken fled indoors and leapt into a tub of cold water. He had received a few stings and decided to remain in bed for three days. Ayah took his meals to him on a tray.

'I didn't know Uncle Ken could run so fast,' I said later that day.

'It's nature's way of compensating,' said Granny.

'What's compensating?'

'Making up for things . . . Now at least Uncle Ken knows that he can run. Isn't that wonderful?'

'It's high time you found a job,' said Granny to Uncle Ken one day.

'There are no jobs in Dehra,' complained Uncle Ken.

'How can you tell? You've never looked for one. And anyway, you don't have to stay here forever. Your sister Emily is the headmistress of a school in Lucknow. You could go to her. She said before that she was ready to put you in charge of a dormitory.'

'Bah!' said Uncle Ken. 'Honestly, you don't expect me to look after a dormitory seething with forty or fifty demented small boys?'

'What's demented?' I asked.

'Shut up,' said Uncle Ken.

'It means crazy,' said Granny.

'So many words mean crazy,' I complained. 'Why don't we just say crazy? We have a crazy dog, and now Uncle Ken is crazy too.'

Uncle Ken clipped me over my ear, and Granny said, 'Your uncle isn't crazy, so don't be disrespectful. He's just lazy.'

'And eccentric,' I said. 'I heard he was eccentric.'

'Who said I was eccentric?' demanded Uncle Ken.

'Miss Leslie,' I lied. I knew Uncle Ken was fond of Miss Leslie, who ran a beauty parlour in Dehra's smart shopping centre, Astley Hall.

'I don't believe you,' said Uncle Ken. 'Anyway, when did you see Miss Leslie?'

'Mohan and I sold her a bottle of Granny's mint chutney last week. I told her you liked mint chutney. But she said she'd bought it for Mr Brown, who's taking her to the pictures tomorrow.'

To our surprise, Uncle Ken got a part-time job as a guide, showing tourists the 'sights' around Dehra.

There was an old fort near the riverbed; and a seventeenth-century temple; and a jail where Pandit Nehru had spent some time as a political prisoner; and, about ten miles into the foothills, the hot sulphur springs.

Uncle Ken told us he was taking a party of six American tourists—husbands and wives—to the sulphur springs. Granny was pleased. Uncle Ken was busy at last! She gave him a hamper filled with ham sandwiches, home-made biscuits and a dozen oranges—ample provision for a day's outing.

The sulphur springs were only ten miles from Dehra, but we didn't see Uncle Ken for three days.

He was a sight when he got back. His clothes were dusty and torn; his cheeks were sunken; and the little bald patch on top of his head had been burnt a bright red.

'What have you been doing to yourself?' asked Granny.

Uncle Ken sank into the armchair on the veranda.

'I'm starving, Mother. Give me something to eat.'

'What happened to the food you took with you?'

'There were seven of us, and it was all finished on the first day.'

'Well, it was only supposed to last a day. You said you were going to the sulphur springs.'

'Yes, that's where we were going,' said Uncle Ken. 'But we never reached them. We got lost in the hills.'

'How could you possibly have got lost in the hills? You had only to walk straight along the riverbed and up the valley . . . You ought to know; you were the guide and you'd been there before, when your father was alive.'

'Yes, I know,' said Uncle Ken, looking crestfallen. 'But I forgot the way. That is, I forgot the valley. I mean, I took them up the wrong valley. And I kept thinking the springs would be at the same river, but it wasn't the same river . . . So we kept walking, until we were in the hills, and then I looked down and saw we'd come up the wrong valley. We had to spend the night under the stars. It was very, very cold. And the next day I thought we'd come back a quicker way, through Mussoorie, but we took the wrong path and reached Kempti instead . . . And then we walked down to the motor road and caught a bus.'

I helped Granny put Uncle Ken to bed and then helped her make him a strengthening onion soup. I took him the soup on a tray, and he made a face while eating it and then asked for more. He was in bed for two days, while Ayah and I took turns taking him his meals. He wasn't a bit grateful.

'We'll have to do something about Uncle Ken,' said Granny to the world at large.

I was in the kitchen with her, shelling peas and popping a few into my mouth now and then. Suzie, the Siamese cat, sat on the sideboard, patiently watching Granny prepare an Irish stew. Suzie liked Irish stew.

'It's not that I mind him staying,' said Granny, 'and I don't want any money from him, either. But it isn't healthy for a young man to remain idle for so long.'

'Is Uncle Ken a young man, Gran?'

'He's thirty. Everyone says he'll improve as he grows up.'

'He could go and live with Aunt Mabel.'

'He *does* go and live with Aunt Mabel. He also lives with Aunt Emily and Aunt Beryl. That's his trouble—he has too many doting sisters ready to put him up and put up with him . . . Their husbands are all quite well off and can afford to have him now and then. So our Ken spends three months with Mabel, three months with Beryl, three months with me. That way he gets by as everyone's guest and doesn't have to worry about making a living.'

'He's lucky, in a way,' I said.

'His luck won't last forever. Already Mabel is talking of going to New Zealand. And once India is free—in just a year or two from now—Emily and Beryl will probably go off to England, because their husbands are in the army and all the British officers will be leaving.'

'Can't Uncle Ken follow them to England?'

'He knows he'll have to start working if he goes there. When your aunts find they have to manage without servants, they won't be ready to keep Ken for long periods. In any case, who's going to pay his fare to England or New Zealand?'

'If he can't go, he'll stay here with you, Granny. You'll be here, won't you?'

'Not forever. Only while I live.'

'You won't go to England?'

'No, I've grown up here. I'm like the trees. I've taken root, I won't be going away—not until, like an old tree, I'm without any more leaves . . . You'll go, though, when you are bigger. You'll probably finish your schooling abroad.'

'I'd rather finish it here. I want to spend all my holidays with you. If I go away, who'll look after you when you grow old?'

'I'm old already. Over sixty.'

'Is that very old? It's only a little older than Uncle Ken. And how will you look after him when you're *really* old?'

'He can look after himself if he tries. And it's time he started. It's time he took a job.'

I pondered over the problem. I could think of nothing that would suit Uncle Ken—or rather, I could think of no one who would find him suitable. It was Ayah who made a suggestion.

'The maharani of Jetpur needs a tutor for her children,' she said. 'Just a boy and a girl.'

'How do you know?' asked Granny.

'I heard it from their ayah. The pay is 200 rupees a month, and there is not much work—only two hours every morning.'

'That should suit Uncle Ken,' I said.

'Yes, it's a good idea,' said Granny. 'We'll have to talk him into applying. He ought to go over and see them. The maharani is a good person to work for.'

Uncle Ken agreed to go over and inquire about the job. The maharani was out when he called, but he was interviewed by the maharaja.

'Do you play tennis?' asked the maharaja.

'Yes,' said Uncle Ken, who remembered having played a bit of tennis when he was a schoolboy.

'In that case, the job's yours. I've been looking for a fourth player for a doubles match . . . By the way, were you at Cambridge?'

'No, I was at Oxford,' said Uncle Ken.

The maharaja was impressed. An Oxford man who could play tennis was just the sort of tutor he wanted for his children.

When Uncle Ken told Granny about the interview, she said, 'But you haven't been to Oxford, Ken. How could you say that!'

'Of course I have been to Oxford. Don't you remember? I spent two years there with your brother Jim!'

'Yes, but you were helping him in his pub in the town. You weren't at the university.'

'Well, the maharaja never asked me if I had been to the university. He asked me if I was at Cambridge, and I said no, I was at Oxford, which was perfectly true. He didn't ask me what I was doing at Oxford. What difference does it make?'

And he strolled off, whistling.

To our surprise, Uncle Ken was a great success at his job. In the beginning, anyway. The maharaja was such a poor tennis player that he was delighted to discover that there was someone who was even worse. So, instead of becoming a doubles partner for the maharaja, Uncle Ken became his favourite singles opponent. As long as he could keep losing to His Highness, Uncle Ken's job was safe.

Between tennis matches and accompanying his employer on duck shoots, Uncle Ken squeezed in a few lessons for the children, teaching them reading, writing and arithmetic. Sometimes he took me along, so that I could tell him when he got his sums wrong. Uncle Ken wasn't very good at subtraction, although he could add fairly well.

The maharaja's children were smaller than me. Uncle Ken would leave me with them, saying, 'Just see that they do their sums properly, Ruskin', and he would stroll off to the tennis courts, hands in his pockets, whistling tunelessly.

Even if his pupils had different answers to the same sum, he would give both of them an encouraging pat, saying, 'Excellent, excellent. I'm glad to see both of you trying so hard. One of you is right and one of you is wrong, but as I don't want to discourage either of you, I won't say who's right and who's wrong!'

But afterwards, on the way home, he'd ask me, 'Which was the right answer, Ruskin?'

Uncle Ken always maintained that he would never have lost his job if he hadn't beaten the maharaja at tennis.

Not that Uncle Ken had any intention of winning.

But by playing occasional games with the maharaja's secretaries and guests, his tennis had improved and so, try as hard as he might to lose, he couldn't help winning a match against his employer.

The maharaja was furious.

'Mr Clerke,' he said sternly, 'I don't think you realize the importance of losing. We can't all win, you know. Where would the world be without losers?'

'I'm terribly sorry,' said Uncle Ken. 'It was just a fluke, Your Highness.'

The maharaja accepted Uncle Ken's apology, but a week later it happened again. Kenneth Clerke won and the maharaja stormed off the court without saying a word. The following day he turned up at lesson time.

As usual, Uncle Ken and the children were engaged in a game of noughts and crosses.

'We won't be requiring your services from tomorrow, Mr Clerke. I've asked my secretary to give you a month's salary in lieu of notice.'

Uncle Ken came home with his hands in his pockets, whistling cheerfully.

'You're early,' said Granny.

'They don't need me any more,' said Uncle Ken.

'Oh, well, never mind. Come in and have your tea.'

Granny must have known the job wouldn't last very long. And she wasn't one to nag. As she said later, 'At least he tried. And it lasted longer than most of his jobs—two months.'

A few days later, he announced that he was going to Lucknow to stay with Aunt Emily. 'She has three children and a school to look after,' said Granny. 'Don't stay too long.'

'She doesn't mind how long I stay,' said Uncle Ken, and off he went.

His visit to Lucknow was a memorable one, and we only heard about it much later.

When Uncle Ken got down at Lucknow station, he found himself surrounded by a large crowd, everyone waving to him and shouting words of welcome in Hindi, Urdu and English. Before he could make out what it was all about, he was smothered by garlands of marigolds. A young man came forward and announced, 'The Gomti Cricketing Association welcomes you to the historical city of Lucknow', and promptly led Uncle Ken out of the station to a waiting car.

It was only when the car drove into the sports stadium that Uncle Ken realized that he was expected to play in a cricket match.

This is what had happened.

Bruce Hallam, the famous English cricketer, was touring India and had agreed to play in a charity match at Lucknow. But the previous evening, in Delhi, Bruce had gone to bed with an upset stomach and hadn't been able to get up in time to catch the train. A telegram was sent to the organizers of the match in Lucknow, but, like many a telegram, it did not reach its destination.

The cricket fans of Lucknow had arrived at the station in droves to welcome the great cricketer. And by a strange coincidence, Uncle Ken bore a startling resemblance to Bruce Hallam—even the bald patch on the crown of his head was exactly like Hallam's. Hence the muddle. And, of course, Uncle Ken was always happy to enter into the spirit of a muddle.

Having received from the Gomti Cricketing Association a rousing reception and a magnificent breakfast at the stadium, he felt that it would be very unsporting on his part if he refused to play cricket for them. *If I can hit a tennis ball*, he mused, *I ought to be able to hit a cricket ball*. And luckily there was a blazer and a pair of white flannels in his suitcase.

The Gomti team won the toss and decided to bat.

Uncle Ken was expected to go in at number three, Bruce Hallam's normal position. And he soon found himself walking to the wicket, wondering why on earth no one had as yet invented a more comfortable kind of pad.

The first ball he received was short-pitched, and he was able to deal with it in tennis fashion, swatting it to the midwicket boundary. He got no runs, but the crowd cheered.

The next ball took Uncle Ken on the pad. He was right in front of his wicket and should have been given out lbw. But the umpire hesitated to raise his finger.

After all, hundreds of people had paid good money to see Bruce Hallam play, and it would have been a shame to disappoint them. 'Not out,' said the umpire.

The third ball took the edge of Uncle Ken's bat and sped through the slips.

'Lovely shot!' exclaimed an elderly gentleman in the pavilion.

'A classic late cut,' said another. The ball reached the boundary and Uncle Ken had four runs to his name. Then it was 'over', and the other batsman had to face the bowling. He took a run off the first ball and called for a second run.

Uncle Ken thought one run was more than enough. Why go charging up and down the wicket like a madman? However, he couldn't refuse to run, and he was halfway down the pitch when the fielder's throw hit the wicket. Uncle Ken was run out by yards. There could be no doubt about it this time.

He returned to the pavilion to the sympathetic applause of the crowd.

'Not his fault,' said the elderly gentleman. 'The other chap shouldn't have called. There wasn't a run there. Still, it was worth coming here all the way from Kanpur, if only to see that superb late cut . . .'

Uncle Ken enjoyed a hearty tiffin, and then, realizing that the Gomti team would probably have to be in the field for most of the afternoon—more running about!—he slipped out of the pavilion, left the stadium and took a tonga to Aunt Emily's house in the cantonment.

He was just in time for a second lunch (taken at 1 o'clock) with Aunt Emily's family, and it was presumed at the stadium that Bruce Hallam had left early to catch the train to Allahabad, where he was expected to play in another charity match.

Aunt Emily, a forceful woman, fed Uncle Ken for a week, and then put him to work in the boys' dormitory of her school. It was several months before he was able to save up enough money to run away and return to Granny's place.

But he had the satisfaction of knowing that he had helped the great Bruce Hallam add another four runs to his grand aggregate. The scorebook of the Gomti Cricketing Association had recorded his feat for all time: 'B. Hallam, run out, 4.'

The Gomti team lost the match. But, as Uncle Ken would readily admit, where would we be without losers?

This story is an excerpt from 'Life with Uncle Ken', *Crazy Times with Uncle Ken*.

# THE HOLIDAY FRIEND

## Shabnam Minwalla

Tehmina and I were strictly holiday friends.

This would have made perfect sense if we'd lived in cities separated by overnight train journeys or troublesome visas. Instead, we both lived in Bombay—Tehmina a twenty-minute drive away from my house in Colaba—and studied under the same sloping, red-tiled roof of Model High School near Churchgate.

She was a year older and a grade higher than me. We must have spotted each other in those stern mustard corridors a few times a day. But we never stopped to chat.

During the school year, we were strangers.

Then summer arrived, with its ripening mangoes, sunshiny days and golden freedom. Model High School always shut on the third weekend of April. And Tehmina always arrived at her grandmother's house on that very Friday evening, bringing two bags stuffed with fripperies and books, an assortment of madcap ideas, big hugs and bigger enthusiasms.

Ten minutes later, my doorbell would ring the merry rhythm that only one person ever attempted. *Tring tring tringity trong!*

'I think Tehmina's here,' my mother would call.

For me, that was the moment the holidays began. Tehmina and I would exchange matter-of-fact smiles and seamlessly resume the friendship that had been on pause for ten months.

Tehmina was the only child in a wealthy Parsi family full of doting grannies and dashing bachelor uncles. She spent the summer holidays with her Mamaiji while her parents went on cruises, climbed the Eiffel Tower and dined with friends in London.

Mamaiji was Tehmina's mother's mother. She was an elegant lady with silver hair, lemon and peach saris and a passion for mah-jong. She lived in Jeroo Mansion, just three buildings away from my own, in a sprawling apartment crowded with mahogany sideboards, crystal bowls and two grand pianos. She kept one room just for Tehmina. In it, Tehmina had a wide desk, a massive cupboard and a carved dressing table topped with an oval mirror. The orange-and-green bedspread with its lush tropical pattern was a perfect match for the curtains hanging at the two windows. The room was our refuge during scorching summer afternoons—dim, cool and messy.

Tehmina's world was impossibly sophisticated compared to my own humdrum existence. My building, Kotak House, daren't even pretend that it was a mansion. I was squished into a room with my brother. There was no space for extras like dressing tables, with or without oval mirrors. Our bedspreads matched nothing except our budget.

Even so, Tehmina and I slipped into each other's lives with ease. I adored the silence of Jeroo Mansion. She thrived in the noise of Kotak House. But the glue in our friendship was a passion for books and a fondness for flights of fancy. I badly wanted to be a writer, and Tehmina badly wanted me to be one.

Every holiday had its theme. One year, we woke up at dawn daily and cycled to the Gateway of India (often imagining that we were being chased by innocent *pavwallas* or indifferent tourists).

Another year, we cut out recipes from *Femina*. Then we pushed Mamaiji's cook, a kind, bulldog-like man named Roderick, out of his kitchen and tried our hand at inedible fruit salads and cookies.

The next year, we played badminton for hours and mooned over cricketers from a visiting team.

There was, however, one ritual that remained constant. Every summer, on that glorious first day when two full months of freedom stretched out before us, we would stroll down the lane and make a left turn on to Colaba Causeway. Then we would cross the main road and arrive at The Causeway Library.

The Causeway Library may sound grand, but don't be misled by the name. This particular establishment was a one-man, one-box affair.

The one man was Mack. A tall, stern individual who reigned over a handkerchief-sized patch of pavement. The one box was a clunky metal affair, about the size of a short, stout refrigerator.

Mack would usually arrive at 11.20 a.m. from his home in the distant suburbs. He'd fish out a heavy key from his pocket and unlock the metal box. After this, he'd scoop out books from its belly. Some he'd arrange on shelves. Others—romances with names like *Summer of Love* and *Moonlight Sonata*—he'd just pile on the lid. He knew they would be in great demand. They always were.

Within minutes, people would arrive. Young housewives and middle-aged secretaries, eager to swap a love story set on a Greek island for a love story set in an English manor. Chatty grannies who browsed for an hour before bearing away gory crime novels. Schoolchildren of all shapes and sizes.

With the nonchalance of a wizard, Mack would pull out frayed and yellowing books to fulfil every demand. *Five on a Secret Trail. The Bobbsey Twins in the Country. The Spy Who Loved Me. Not a Penny More, Not a Penny Less. The Thorn Birds. The Far Pavilions.*

When he couldn't find a particular book, he'd scribble the name in his Navneet notebook, promise to hunt for it and supply an 'even better' substitute. All day, people walked away from The Causeway Library with smiles and armloads of yellow books. And like them, we were addicted to the paperback goodies and haphazard magic of The Causeway Library.

Nowadays, I visit bookshops and libraries where collections are arranged by author, by genre, by levels. The Causeway Library was the very opposite. When Mack pulled out handfuls of books from his box, you never knew what would emerge. Amidst the Enid Blytons would be a philosophical ramble written by a Britisher in Mahabaleshwar. Or paperbacks with names like *Purple Passion*, about cruel pirates and damsels whose violet eyes flashed fire.

Sandwiched between the Archie's Digests were unexpected offerings like *Zen and the Art of Motorcycle Maintenance*. (Not meant for your average Archie reader, but we read it anyway. Tehmina even claimed that she understood it. I certainly didn't.)

This was part of the charm of The Causeway Library. We never knew quite what would come out of that metal repository. But one thing we did know—once a book went back into the box, it was almost impossible to locate it. This was why we'd grab anything that looked remotely promising.

Over those summers the books we borrowed mapped our lives. Judy and Bunty comics, and Secret Seven adventures. Then Nancy Drew and

Hardy Boys mysteries. After which came books packed with adventure and mystery, like *The Scarlet Pimpernel* and Sherlock Holmes.

The year that came after the *Scarlet Pimpernel* summer was a turbulent one. I squabbled with my mother. My best friend of many years had drifted away, leaving me lonely and insecure. But worst was the fact that Miss Coutinho, our prune-faced, arsenic-hearted class teacher, took pleasure in tormenting me. She was a bully, who picked on a couple of students every year. That year, I was her victim.

She jeered at my questions in history. She ripped my maps in geography. But most shattering, she mocked my English essays. She circled my phrases with a screaming orange pen and read them out in class in a scornful voice; she urged my mother to restrict my reading to 'beneficial books'.

The dream of becoming a writer wilted beneath her toxic scorn.

To complete the cliche of the troubled teenager, I was batty over a boy from Jeroo Mansion. Rohan was already in college, mad about motorcycles and had no time for shy schoolgirls.

I was busy wallowing in self-pity when Tehmina rang the doorbell on the last day of that dreadful academic year. My welcome was muted. Everything bugged me. The heat, the pimple on my chin, my unfashionably long blue dress.

Not that Tehmina was bothered. She bounced into our house, teased my brother, chattered with my mother about Mamaiji's cataract operation and then turned to me. 'How many chapters done?' she asked.

The previous summer—our *Scarlet Pimpernel* summer—we'd started working on our very own adventure novel. It was set in Mumbai. To be more precise, it was set in Colaba and featured two marvellous male protagonists: a young Hollywood star and the son of an Italian count with a palace in Venice. (There were very good reasons for them to be wandering around Colaba Causeway helping two Bombay schoolgirls catch diamond thieves. But I've forgotten those reasons now.)

We'd written six chapters. Then school had played spoilsport. Tehmina had left the manuscript with me. 'Just in case you get ideas,' she'd said. 'After all, you're the writer.'

But I was the writer no longer. Tehmina's question poked at my worries. 'No progress,' I said with a scowl. 'I don't think I can write any more. I can barely manage a sentence these days.'

Tehmina laughed. 'We'll work on it together,' she said. 'And don't talk rubbish.'

The next morning we set out for The Causeway Library. After a long time, I felt close to happy. Tehmina told me that her parents had gone to Germany and had almost taken her along but finally went with friends instead. I mentioned Rohan. Very casually, I thought. But my blush gave me away.

'What are you not telling me?' Tehmina demanded. 'Who's this Rohan? One of those noisy boys that Mamaiji's always complaining about? The one who keeps patting his hair? Or the one who wears pink shirts?'

When we encountered Rohan and his gang on our way to get Chocobars that evening, Tehmina was not impressed. 'Him?' she squawked in disparaging tones, sounding alarmingly like Mamaiji. 'He's so ordinary. Not a patch on Francesco Corti. Or the Scarlet Pimpernel.'

In case you're wondering, Francesco Corti was the son of the Italian count. He had quick wits, incredible boxing skills and a charming smile.

I pointed out that both Francesco Corti and the Scarlet Pimpernel were fictional characters. But Tehmina snorted. 'It's the principle of the matter,' she insisted. 'You can't be nuts over someone like that Rohan. I bet *Noddy Goes to Toyland* was the last book he ever read. He's definitely not our type. And his friends are sniggering idiots.'

She stopped to take a ferocious bite of ice cream before continuing. 'What's happened to you, Malu? You have to aim for something special. You have to start writing again. You have to stay the person that you are. Promise me.'

I promised, but it was an empty promise. I remained sad and full of self-doubt. I felt sure I could never be a writer.

This went on for three weeks. Till the day we visited The Causeway Library and returned with *The Weeping Willow* by Doris Delaney.

Tehmina ate lunch at our house that day after our jaunt to the library and had a high-spirited tiff with my brother. Then we went across to Jeroo Mansion to work on our novel. On the way I announced that the son of the Italian count and the Hollywood star needed to be replaced by more realistic heroes.

Tehmina was shocked. She was not a girl who gave up on dreams.

We snapped at each other till Tehmina suddenly said, 'Okay. I have an idea. I read a book in which there was a girl called Abigail who had no one to properly talk to. So whenever she was really confused about what to do, she would open a book to a random page. And she would find her answer. Let's do that. Let's ask a book what we should do about our heroes.'

Even by Tehmina's whimsical standards, this was a strange idea. 'What rubbish,' I protested. 'That's impossible. How can a book provide a proper answer?'

'Not exact answers,' Tehmina explained. 'But the book gave Abigail general directions. You know, like whether Abigail should sail to China or Japan or somewhere.'

'And what did the book say?' I asked, fascinated despite myself.

'Oh, the book told her to go,' Tehmina said with a giggle. 'But that's not important. What I found really interesting was how she asked the book for help. She followed strict rules—only three questions at a time. And only when she had three really, really important questions. What do you think?'

I shrugged. I felt both sceptical and intrigued. 'We can try,' I said. 'Though I bet it won't work.'

'Bet it will,' Tehmina countered and grabbed a book at random. It was *Anne of Green Gables*, which made us smile. We both adored Anne, the carrot-haired orphan with the irrepressible imagination and knack for getting into scrapes.

Holding the book, Tehmina sat on the green-and-orange bedspread. I sat next to her and waited. 'Okay, three questions,' Tehmina announced, placing the book on her lap. 'The first question is about our book. You ask.'

'Okay,' I said, feeling a bit foolish. 'Here's my question: Is there any point in writing a story that is so completely impossible? Shouldn't we write something more . . . sensible?'

Tehmina hated all things 'sensible'. She wrinkled her nose, opened the book to a random page and crowed with glee. 'Look at what Anne has to say. You know the bit where she first meets Matthew and she imagines herself wearing a pale-blue silk dress and a big hat with nodding plumes? Guess what she says.'

'I can't guess,' I said. 'Just read it out.'

'Okay,' Tehmina said, twinkling. 'She says, "Because when you are imagining, you might as well imagine something worthwhile."'

Tehmina was convinced, but I was not. 'We only got our answer because you picked *Anne of Green Gables*,' I protested. 'I bet another book wouldn't have an answer.'

'You try with another book,' Tehmina said. 'Pick a book we've never read before. One of the library books. I have something important to ask.'

I leaned across and picked up a book from the Causeway Library pile. The cover must once have been the bright green of spring but had now achieved the dull hue of scorched grass. It was called *The Weeping Willow*, but there was no blurb to tell us what lay between the flaking, fading covers.

'Ask,' I said.

Tehmina looked suddenly sad as she gazed at the book in my hand. 'I keep wondering, will I ever have a proper family?' she asked. 'Parents who eat dinner with me? Who want to travel with me? Who are interested in what I do at school?'

I felt a jolt of astonishment. In all these years I'd never imagined that Tehmina was unhappy with her grand life. I opened the book, unsure about what I was looking for till I saw it—a paragraph in the middle of a conversation between somebody called Eileen and somebody called Henri.

'You can't choose the family you were born into,' I read aloud. 'But you can choose your friends. So stop fretting about the family you were born with, and instead work towards the family that you will one day live with. Build it one friend at a time.'

Tehmina was silent for a beat. Then she rubbed her eyes briskly and shook her head hard so that her brown curls bounced. 'That's not the answer I wanted. But it makes sense. Some things can't be changed and controlled, and I guess my family's one of those. So, instead, I'll choose the best possible friends. Actually, I already have.'

She leaned over and gave me one of her vanilla-scented hugs. And though I was not a touchy-feely person, this time I hugged her back. Tightly.

'Okay, your turn, Malu,' Tehmina announced, taking *The Weeping Willow* from me.

I was about to ask a question about Rohan, but Tehmina pre-empted me. 'Don't you dare waste your question on that duffer,' she warned. 'Ask about your writing. That's the most important thing of all.'

I was about to protest—till I saw Tehmina's serious, intent expression. 'Ummm . . . should I believe Miss Coutinho?' I mumbled, feeling suddenly nervous. 'Am I horrible at writing? Should I stop trying to be a writer? Is it a ridiculous ambition?'

Tehmina opened the book, peered at the page and broke into a broad smile. 'Just listen to this, Malu,' she said before she started reading. 'Don't ever let small minds and smaller hearts convince you that your dreams are too big.'

Tehmina shut the book with a firm snap and clapped her hands. 'There's nobody in the world who has a smaller mind and smaller heart than Creepy Coutinho. Now, whenever you see her, imagine her with a brain the size of a pea and a heart the size of a mustard seed.'

I laughed. And in that magical moment, Miss Coutinho lost her terrible power over me. I was free to dream again.

Tehmina and I never did read *The Weeping Willow*. We tried, but realized that pages in the middle were missing. It was impossible to make sense of the story. So we returned it to the library.

(Later, it struck me that Tehmina had been particularly anxious to return the book without reading it. Over the years I've often wondered if she made up that little nugget of wisdom, just to perk me up.)

Strangely, or maybe not strangely, I never encountered *The Weeping Willow* again. Neither at The Causeway Library nor at any future library or bookstore I ever visited. Not even on the Internet, though I've checked time and again.

Still, the book had done its job.

We completed our adventure novel and, once the holidays ended, our friends enjoyed it. When we passed each other in school, we started to exchange nods and smiles.

Tehmina made many friends, and keeps in touch with all of them. She even married one of them and now has three boisterous, loving children. We meet often, and not just during the holidays. And whenever we talk about that summer, Tehmina always says that *The Weeping Willow* saved her from resentment and bitterness. 'It was like a road sign. You know, one of those that say, "Danger Ahead. Take a Detour." Lucky I spotted it just in time.'

As for me, well, if you're reading this, you know that I actually became a writer. All thanks to a fat metal box, a book with a flaking cover and a friend who believed in me even when I stopped believing in myself.

SO WHAT DID
THE GOD SAY?

Subhadra Sen Gupta

My sister, Durga, raised her huge eyes to my father's face and asked, 'Do we have to work in Puri, Babu?'

Babu shook his head. 'No. We are going on a pilgrimage.'

'No work at all?'

'No work, just a holiday at the rath yatra.'

Durga curved her head to smile at me, where I was sitting behind her. 'Imagine, Kartik Dada, our first holiday!'

Ma and Babu laughed.

I stretched my legs out, leaned back against the rounded thatched covering of the bullock cart and looked up at the sky. The sun was still an orange half-circle on the horizon, the sky fading into a pale blue, and the trees bordering the fields had changed from black to a shadowy charcoal grey. Then a streak of sunlight touched the edge of a cloud with a fleeting wash of pink and mauve.

I notice colours; you do when you spend your days around coloured threads and a weaver's loom.

We were going to Puri with a cartload of saris and dhotis that Babu would sell in the temple town. Usually he travelled with other weavers from our village, like my friend Murari's father, but this time Ma, Durga and I were going with him. It was the monsoon month of Ashadh and the time of the rath yatra at the Jagannath Temple. Durga and I had never seen the chariot festival.

Durga chattered on, 'Does Lord Jagannath drive his chariot?'

Babu shook his head. 'Images of Jagannath, his brother, Balabhadra, and sister, Subhadra, are put in the chariots and people pull them with ropes.'

*How can any god or goddess drive a chariot?* I thought. *They are made of wood or stone and can't move.*

'Where are they going?' Durga asked.

'To the Gundicha Temple at the other end of the main road, called Bada Danda, where their aunt stays. They come back ten days later.'

'So they are on holiday too.'

'They are always on holiday,' I said softly to myself so that Babu couldn't hear me. 'When do our gods do any work?'

Ma, sitting in front of me, gave me a warning glance. Today I was not to talk like this and upset Babu, who worshipped Jagannath every day.

In our family all we knew was work. I helped Babu with the weaving. We had to dye the threads and dry them along the bamboo fence in our courtyard. Then we laid the threads along the loom, and Babu would bend over the loom all day weaving the threads of the weft and warp until, like magic, a sari began to appear before him in iridescent colours and delicate patterns. I was learning on a smaller loom and had woven my first bundle of dhotis. I loved drawing new patterns for the borders and *pallav*, and my favourite was the curving motif called *ambi*, which was shaped like a mango.

While Babu and I worked at the loom, Ma and Durga did all the housework—fetching water from the pond, milking the cow, tending the vegetable garden, cooking, washing clothes and cleaning the pots and pans. Our work never ended. I was fourteen, Durga was nine and we worked all the time, except when we went to school. Puri was just a day's ride from our village, but for a poor weaver's family it was just too far.

As we neared Puri, the road began to get crowded with bullock carts; some carried pilgrims heading for the rath yatra, others were piled with goods—pottery and toys, leather and wood ware, fruits and vegetables. Occasionally a crowded bus rattled past.

'On the day of the yatra we have to get up early,' Ma said. 'I want to stand somewhere from where I can see the chariots and the idols.'

'I know a place,' Babu said. 'One of the shops that sell my saris stands right on the main road. The last time I was here during the yatra, the shopkeeper let me sit on the roof, and I could see straight into the chariots.'

Ma smiled. 'Oh, good! After all, this is the only time in the year that we can get a darshan of the deities. If I can see them with my own eyes, I know that my prayers will be answered.'

'Only time in the year?' I asked, puzzled. 'If you want to do puja and a darshan, why don't we go to the temple?'

There was a small silence and then Ma said, 'You know we won't be allowed inside.'

Durga turned to stare at Ma. 'Why?'

'Only the higher castes are allowed inside the sanctum, the *garbhagriha*, where the idols stand, not people like us—farmers, weavers, potters . . .'

'Poor people,' Durga said, nodding. She understood very well.

'Since we cannot go see the deities in the temple, Lord Jagannath comes out once a year so we can all pray to him.'

*So kind of him*, I thought.

I once heard Ma tell Babu that they shouldn't have sent me to the village school. I was getting all sorts of wrong ideas from our teacher Jiten da. He was very different from the priest, Ponditmoshai, who ran a pathshala at the temple. He would have made us memorize Sanskrit slokas, while Jiten da was teaching us algebra and geography and talking about Gandhiji and freedom.

As our village was quite big, the government built a school, and one day Jiten da came to teach there. He wore khadi kurtas and pyjamas instead of a dhoti and a sacred thread, and he did not have a shaven head or a *shikha*, that ridiculous long strand of hair at the back of the head. People said he did not look like a teacher at all. Everyone could join this school, and no one checked your jati or *gotra*. The Brahmin boys, of course, did not come, as they refused to sit next to us. Ponditmoshai had said that the world would come to an end because the children of leather workers and farm labourers were touching the sacred books.

Jiten da had grinned and retorted, 'I am teaching them to read and write in Odia, mathematics, history and geography. Sanskrit is not in the syllabus.'

Murari and I were in class eight, and we had dropped in at Jiten da's home the day before to tell him about our trip to Puri. He was reading the newspaper and said anxiously, 'They have arrested Pandit Nehru again.'

'Gandhiji has been arrested too?'

Jiten da shook his head. He was the only person in the village who got the newspaper from Puri, and a few months earlier we had breathlessly followed the Dandi March led by Gandhiji. Jiten da was not teaching us Sanskrit slokas; instead, he was teaching us how to be free. Our fathers did not know about this, of course.

We were going to stay in an old dharamshala on the outskirts of the city as the rooms were cheap. When we entered the inn we discovered that Murari and his family had already arrived. Next morning, as our fathers headed to the market with the saris and dhotis, Murari and I hitched a ride and jumped off at the main road before the temple. We were going to see the famous Jagannath Temple for the first time in our lives.

We looked around in amazement. What a sight! The broad road was lined with shops bright with goods and shelves of cloth in all the colours of the rainbow; baskets and pottery were stacked by doors; food shops were serving delicious sweets and snacks; and cooks were stirring food in large pans over smoking fires. We wandered down, peering into a jeweller's shop, a stall where a pretty woman was selling paan and a flower shop that had fragrant garlands swaying in the breeze. The whole place was teeming with people.

'Look! The temple!' Murari shouted. We stood and stared at the largest temple we had ever seen.

I couldn't believe that human beings had built such a magnificent shrine. The ancient Jagannath Temple stood behind high walls, and from the road all we could see were the shikharas, the triangular spires. There were two smaller shikharas and then a tall one at the end with a huge flag snapping in the breeze. The shikharas were carved and painted white, gleaming in the sun. Then we noticed the three wooden chariots standing before the main gate. They had brightly coloured cloth canopies, and the wheels were taller than us. The yatra was just a few days away, and work was still going on. A carpenter was hammering away at a wooden pillar; a painter was colouring the carved horses and riders placed in front of the chariot; a boy was attaching marigold garlands to the canopy.

'Which one is Jagannath's?' I wondered out loud.

An old man was standing next to us. He wore a faded dhoti, his body wrapped in a tattered shawl, his feet in old chappals. He had been listening to us. He pointed and said, 'The chariot with the yellow and red canopy, called Nandighosh, is Jagannath's chariot. Subhadra rides Padmadhwaja, with the red and black top, and Balabhadra's chariot is called Taladhwaja and has the red and blue canopy.'

'Aren't Subhadra and Balabhadra the sister and brother of Lord Krishna?' Murari said thoughtfully. 'Then Jagannath is actually Lord Krishna.'

'Correct.' He looked amused at our questions.

'Sir, do you live here?' Murari asked.

'Lived in Puri all my life.'

'Then can you explain something? Our fathers are weavers, and my friend here says that we are not allowed inside the temple because of our caste. But I see craftsmen like us working inside the chariots. So he is mistaken, isn't he?'

'Your friend is right. They need the craftsmen now to build the chariots because the priests would never pick up a hammer or a paintbrush. When their work is done the craftsmen will have to step away while the priests place the idols inside the chariots. They won't be allowed to ride with the deities or even put flowers before them. Just like the stone sculptors who create statues of gods but cannot touch them once they are placed in the sanctum. Their touch is then considered dirty.'

'How is that possible? It is the sculptors who carved the image.'

'The priests say if we lower castes touch them, the gods will curse us.'

'Why do people believe them?'

'Because people are poor, and they are afraid of the kings and the priests.'

Murari looked around. 'Suppose we just went inside? It's so crowded they wouldn't be able to catch us.'

'Oh, you can go inside the temple. They'll stop you at the door of the garbhagriha, the sanctum where the idols stand. The guards will spot you.'

'How will they know I'm not an upper caste?'

The old man laughed. 'No sacred thread, shaven head or shikha like a Brahman. No silk dhoti or jewellery like the rich. You look poor. Do you know that even the devadasis who dance before Jagannath are not allowed to touch the images? We all have to stand like beggars at the door of the sanctum and give our offerings to the priest.'

'If they do the puja, they keep the money,' I said.

'Exactly! It's all about the money.'

'That's why they want to keep us uneducated.'

He stared at me. 'You go to school?'

I nodded. 'Good. Get educated so that one day you can join Gandhiji and fight to enter the garbhagriha.'

'I think we'll try today,' Murari said with a thoughtful frown.

The old man shook his head disbelievingly, laughed and walked away.

Murari and I stood across the road from the main gate of the temple, and I asked, 'You're serious about going in today?'

'I am. If we get caught, we'll act like stupid villagers, say we got lost, then weep and apologize, and I'm sure they'll let us go.'

I grinned at his description of us as stupid villagers because that is what the city people expect. I was studying the high wall and the people around the main gate and spotted two guards with sticks, watching the pilgrims going in. 'Such a huge temple. There must be other gates . . .'

We strolled along the walls, went round the corners and found at the back wall a smaller gate that was not guarded. It seemed to be used by people who worked inside the temple and was busy with activity. Men were unloading jars of ghee from a cart, and some other workers were carrying in bundles of firewood from a pile that had been unloaded beside the gate.

'Hey! You two!' a man who stood beside the firewood stack suddenly yelled at us. 'Carry the firewood inside to the kitchen.'

'How much will you pay us?' I asked.

'Two paise for every load you carry in.'

The wood seller pointed at a building. 'Follow that man and put the wood outside the kitchen door.'

Being village people, both of us had the red-and-white checked *gamocha* cloth tied like a scarf around our necks. We quickly tied the gamocha around our heads so that our hair was completely covered. Now no one could guess that we did not have the shaven head of a Brahman. We walked in slowly, looking around the precinct. We were in the back courtyard, which had many small halls with carved pillars, and the place was crowded with pilgrims. No one gave us a second glance.

We added the wood to a huge stack at the door of the kitchen and then very carefully peered inside. It was like looking into the mouth of a volcano—the heat of a hundred open *chullahs* came pouring out of the door and made us sweat. The open ovens stood in rows, with cooks bending over large pots and pans smoking with ghee; other ovens had tall stacks of earthen pots placed one on top of the other. The air smelled of frying masala, boiling milk and hot ghee. In this smoky, sweaty melee men moved around like ghosts, yelling at each other.

Then one of the cooks at the other end of the kitchen called out, 'Boys! Bring some firewood here!', and we were in.

We rushed up with an armful of firewood, and I squatted before the chullah and fed the fire with small pieces of wood. The cook was a tall, thin man with a high-cheekboned face. He snapped at Murari, 'Get me some turmeric from that jar there!'

Murari ran up with the jar of turmeric and filled the cook's masala thali.

I peered into a pot of boiling vegetables and asked, 'What are you cooking, sir?'

'Cabbage and peas.' He was busy stirring and adding masalas, sweat dripping down his face. 'Then I have to fry those brinjals with spinach . . .'

'Shall I cut the brinjals?' Murari asked. The cook nodded. Murari sat on the floor, pulled the metal *bonti* closer and began to slice the brinjals.

As I looked around, I noticed something. There was a door on the opposite side of the kitchen, and a man was going through it carrying two baskets with pots of food attached to a bamboo pole. The *bhog* for the deities was being taken to the main temple through that door. I had seen this at our village temple during festivals, when the gods were offered cooked food. In our tiny temple the lords only got bananas and sugar batasha for prasad.

'How many dishes will be cooked today?' I asked.

'Fifty-six. Don't you know anything? This is the *chhappano* bhog for the gods.' He turned to Murari.

'You! Hurry up! The mahaprasad has to be ready by noon for the bhog ceremony.'

As we walked away I said, 'So we have been inside the temple, even seen the kitchen. Let's get out now.'

'Nah!' Murari gave a stubborn shake of his head. 'This was easy. We have to enter the sanctum and meet Lord Jagannath.' He looked around. 'I don't know how, though . . . We can't ask anyone for directions, can we?'

I pointed to the pile of pots collecting near the door. 'We take in the food.'

We walked up casually, bent down and picked up a pot each. One held the milk and rice sweet, payesh, and the other had small til ladoos. One man had just left with his load of baskets, so we followed.

'Don't get too close,' Murari whispered a warning. 'He may see us.' But the man was so heavily laden with pots that he did not look back.

We went through a dingy, dark passage and turned a corner. Suddenly I heard the sounds of a puja taking place—the raised voices of the priests chanting mantras, cymbals clanging, conches being blown. The fifty-six dishes were collecting by a door. We put our pots there, and then, after looking around, we slipped through the narrow door that led into the garbhagriha.

It was a world of noise, incense smoke, chanting, yelling and clapping. The room was quite small, and it was packed with people. We slid into the crowd. When I looked up I saw three idols stood on a high altar, called the *ratnabedi*, where a priest was doing the *arati*, raising and lowering a tall metal lamp with twenty-one flames. I checked to make sure my gamocha still covered my head.

There they stood, the three deities that were adored all across our kingdom: Jagannath, Balabhadra and Subhadra. I knew they were really logs of wood with faces painted on them, but they had a surprising majesty—the wide-open eyes that seemed to stare right back at me and the kind and gentle curving smiles. They were covered in garlands, and people were throwing handfuls of flowers so that the altar was covered in marigolds and rose petals.

After the arati the spectators began to leave through a side door as a curtain was pulled across the altar. The gods were now going to have their lunch. As we walked past the altar, Murari and I grabbed some marigolds and stuffed them in our pockets.

We stood on the road taking huge breaths of relief.

'How is it no one spotted us?' I asked.

Murari was unwrapping the gamocha from his head. 'Thanks to this, and also because we're wearing new clothes.'

'That's all it takes to become a high-caste Hindu?' I laughed. 'A gamocha and new clothes?'

Murari stood still. 'Oh, we forgot to get the money for carrying the wood!' But by the time we went back the woodman was gone.

Our fathers were waiting at the sari shop. As we headed back to the dharamshala in the cart, we told them what we had done, even showing them the marigolds. Neither of them believed us, of course.

'You want me to believe that you went into the kitchen and touched the bhog?' Babu gave me an unconvinced look.

'And you went into the garbhagriha and watched the arati?' Murari's father's voice echoed Babu's.

'And no one stopped you at the door? You weren't spotted inside?'

'The kitchen was so full of smoke that everyone looked like ghosts,' Murari replied.

'We entered the garbhagriha through a side door, and it was packed with people.' I described the arati ceremony in detail, and, finally, Babu began to believe, shaking his head in a mix of happiness and anxiety.

He turned to Murari's father, his eyes glittering with joy. 'Two weaver boys touch the bhog, enter the garbhagriha and pick up the puja flowers . . .'

Murari's father threw back his head and laughed. 'And the world did not come to an end, my friend! Nothing happened!'

As the cart creaked along, Babu grew quiet. Eventually, he said, 'You boys have to promise me something.' Murari and I nodded. 'You will only tell your mothers what you did and no one else. If the temple priests find out, they will complain to the maharaja, and we could be in serious trouble.'

Murari and I nodded again.

Ma listened to me and asked gently, 'So what did the god say to you, Kartik?'

I remembered the wide, watchful eyes and the smile that curved from ear to ear. 'He smiled and said, "Welcome to my kingdom, Kartik!"'

'Really?' She frowned. 'He was not angry with you?'

'No. All three of them just smiled.'

Ma touched the handful of marigolds to her forehead and closed her eyes in prayer. It felt good to have made her so happy.

Historical Note

During our freedom struggle, Mahatma Gandhi also began a campaign against the caste system. He threw away his sacred thread and never did pujas. Instead, he led hartals outside temples that refused entry to the lower castes. Later, our Constitution granted every citizen of India the right to pray anywhere they want. We also have the right not to believe in any religion. The choice is ours.

Think about it. Why would our kind and generous gods and goddesses refuse our offerings? None of our most ancient sacred books like the *Vedas* or the *Upanishads* say that society has to be divided by the castes of varna, jati or gotra. These divisions were created by priests, and they are human, just like us.

A PARROT
NAMED CARROT

Khyrunnisa A.

The whole school was looking forward to summer vacation. What school doesn't? So it came as a great shock when Mrs Susy Joseph, the principal of Stones and Pebbles High School (SAP, for short), announced that they were going to start something new, something . . .

'. . . verrry exciting! Vacation classes!' she trilled and looked keenly at the students, almost urging them to break into thunderous applause. A stony silence greeted the news. Not that she had expected anything different, but she was one of those eternal optimists who never gave up hope that miracles could happen. Except for the fact that her school was located a few kilometres from a prison, which made her a little nervous at times, she was upbeat about life.

She cleared her throat and continued, unfazed, 'Excellent! Remember, this is just an experiment. Most schools have vacation classes. Your parents have been asking me why our school doesn't organize them. They don't want you to be watching TV or be glued to your gadgets all the time. We begin with a ten-day programme, and if it's a success, we'll extend it to a month. Fun classes, children, good, pure fun. You'll learn a little bit of what awaits you in the next academic year, and isn't it wonderful that you'll already know what you're going to learn next year? But it will be done in a different way. There will be no homework, no punishments; it will all be activity-based. And your own teachers will take the classes.'

The hearts of the teachers sank when they heard this. Mrs Joseph had briefed them vaguely about the possibility of vacation classes at the last staff meeting, but borrowing some of her optimism, the teachers had hoped they wouldn't happen, and if they did, it would be invited guests who engaged the classes. The students looked mutinous.

Mrs Joseph continued, 'So, my dear teachers and students, isn't that something to look forward to? Now, children, please march to your classes.' She beat a hasty retreat.

'Our school is SAP, all right,' grumbled Mr Ranjit, the physics teacher, on returning to the staff room. 'Working here saps your energy.'

'Parents can't be bothered to take care of their children during vacations and want us to play nanny,' observed Mr Prasad, the English teacher, looking peeved. 'Very clever!'

The students too mumbled, grumbled and protested all the way to their classes.

'Who wants to learn anything ahead?' whined Mathew of VII B to his friends in class. 'Or even at the right time?'

'Fun classes indeed!' muttered Rajesh. 'There goes my plan of perfecting my ventriloquism during the holidays.'

'Did you say, "perfecting your ventriloquism"?' Savita said, laughing. 'I haven't heard your voice come from anywhere but your own lips, and with great difficulty at that.'

'Ah, listen carefully. Beware! I'll surprise you all one day,' Rajesh hissed through clenched teeth.

'Ha ha, was that the wastepaper basket speaking?' asked Leela with a guffaw. 'I thought it came from Rajesh.'

'Same thing,' Prabhu said with a wink.

Soon the exams rolled up, and school finally came to a close. Well, not exactly, because the vacation classes started.

'Good morning! Good morning!' said Mr Prasad, the English master, in a fake cheerful tone as he entered VII B. He was the class teacher and didn't want his class to suspect that he had probably been more reluctant to come to school than the students.

'Good morning! Come right in! Why are you so late?' a shrill voice responded.

Mr Prasad froze. What were students coming to these days? A vacation class didn't mean students could take liberties with the teachers. He was about to make an angry remark, when a piercing laugh scared him out of his wits. He dropped his book and turned around wildly. The voice now screamed, 'Help! Murder!'

He jumped, tottered against the table and held it for support with trembling hands. The students, who had stood up when he entered, giggled at this virtuoso performance.

*How dare they laugh*, he thought, and getting hold of himself, looked up in anger, straight into the baleful eyes of a parrot perched on the shoulder of a boy in the first row.

'Good morning, sir!' said the boy, with a pleasant smile. 'I'm a new student, Remu, and this is my parrot. Her name is Carrot.'

'What's all this nonsense!' Mr Prasad snapped, now back to his normal self. 'I'm not here to teach carrots, I mean, parrots. Get it out of my sight! I'm going to complain to the principal.' He began to take purposeful strides to the door when, as if on cue, the principal herself entered the class.

'Ah, Prasad! Good morning, children. Please sit down,' Mrs Joseph said, nodding to the students, who were enjoying this drama hugely. Whoever imagined vacation classes could be this exciting? This surpassed all their expectations.

'Hands up!' shrieked Carrot, sending the class into more giggles. Only Mr Prasad wasn't amused.

'Mr Prasad, I wanted to tell you about this new boy and the parrot before you came to class, but I didn't find you in the staffroom,' Mrs Joseph said.

'Late, always late,' muttered the parrot.

The students suppressed their smiles while Mr Prasad blushed. Mrs Joseph pretended not to have heard the remark and, in a low tone, continued, 'So I decided to come to your class. I'm sure you are wondering who this boy is and why he has come here with a parrot. Well, Remu is my nephew, and the parrot belongs to my brother Rajive, Remu's father. Rajive loves his pet and can't bear to be parted from her. But two days back he had severe abdominal pain and was rushed to hospital.'

'Who? The parrot?' asked Meena, who was in the first row and had been straining her ears to listen to this narration. Remu had already told the students the whole story, but she wanted everything to be very clear.

'Of course not. Don't be silly and don't interrupt, my dear girl,' the principal retorted, frowning at Meena.

'And don't eavesdrop.' She continued, 'It was found that Rajive needed an emergency appendicitis surgery, an appendectomy, to be precise. After the surgery there were some minor complications, so he has to be in hospital for at least ten days. His wife is with him, and I said I'd take care of Remu, but the parrot can't be left alone. So I though the parrot could come to school with Remu till my brother returns home.'

'But why can't it be left in a cage at home?' Mr Prasad protested, raising his voice. 'All you need to do is arrange for someone to give it some seeds and it will be fine.' Carrot screamed in protest.

Mr Prasad had once had a parrot that he had treated like this, and at the first opportunity the parrot had bitten his hand viciously and run away, rather, flown away, to freedom. That hadn't taught him a lesson; instead, it had reinforced his opinion that a caged parrot should never be let out. But he couldn't bear the sight of a parrot after that experience. He looked down at a deep scar on his left hand and winced, as if it still hurt.

'No, Prasad, that's impossible,' Mrs Joseph explained. 'She's used to flying freely about. Besides, there's a cat in the neighbourhood that's out to get Princess.'

'Princess?' Mr Prasad looked puzzled.

'Yes, that's her name, but Remu calls her Carrot. I know this is an unusual situation, but I've got special permission from the school's board of directors. It's just for ten days, Prasad, and Princess will be no trouble. Remu, see that she isn't a nuisance to the teachers and doesn't disrupt classes. Thank you, Prasad, I knew you'd understand.' She gave a bright smile and marched out of the room.

Mr Prasad grimaced, but brightened a little when he saw the school cat jump from a tree in the distance. 'Remu,' he hollered, 'you can sit by the open window. Then that wretched creat . . . er, parrot, can fly out whenever it wants.' He hoped the cat would make a meal of the parrot.

Carrot cleared her throat and squawked, 'Shut up!' Mr Prasad glared at her.

'Sir, she doesn't like being called "it". You must say "she",' explained Remu, moving to the seat by the window.

'I suppose I must call her "Your Royal Highness"?' Mr Prasad asked, sarcasm dripping from his voice.

'Else I'll shoot!' Carrot screamed and then cackled.

'I'm sorry, sir.' Remu looked contrite. 'My father watches a lot of thriller movies, and she's picked up many expressions from them. Carrot is very intelligent, sir.'

That was the beginning of a most entertaining time for the students and a traumatic one for Mr Prasad. Strangely enough, Carrot never troubled the other teachers, remaining either quiet or leaving the room when they were in class. Occasionally she amused them with her clever remarks, calling the maths teacher Einstein—'Genius! Einstein returns!'—paying flattering compliments to the attractive history teacher—'Pretty lady, I bow to thee!'—or pretending to be a train when the physics teacher described how a train's engine functioned— 'Pheee! Chug! Chug! Chug! Pheee!' But her best was reserved for Mr Prasad.

She sensed that VII B's class teacher hated her and, responding to this in a way that was almost human, she went out of her way to imitate him, trouble him, startle him or disturb him. The students looked forward to the duels between the two, while Mr Prasad, at the end of his tether, counted the days to the end of this ordeal.

On the ninth day, just as classes were about to begin, the intercom crackled to life and Mrs Joseph's voice came trembling through. She quavered that she had just received an alert from the police. 'A notorious convict has escaped from the nearby prison. Worse, he has managed to steal a gun from a policeman. The police believe he cannot have gone far, and they want everyone to be on their guard. I don't think he'll come here—we are well protected—but please be careful and don't wander out of your classes. Teachers, be especially vigilant.' Her worst fears had come true, and the tremor in her voice as it faded out indicated how much the news had affected her.

'Ooh!' The students were thrilled, and such cacophony erupted from every classroom that Mrs Joseph resorted to the use of the intercom once again, but this time, used a stern, no-nonsense voice and veiled threats to quieten the children.

'Great news!' Carrot screeched at Mr Prasad when he entered the class in the afternoon.

'Shut up!' barked Mr Prasad with a scowl. Unlike the students, the teachers were disturbed by the warning and hoped the convict would be caught soon.

'Not happy? Bad boy! Bang! Bang!' Carrot flew twice around Mr Prasad's head before settling down on Remu's shoulder.

Since the teachers who had taken the morning classes for VII B hadn't allowed any student to ask questions about the jail breakout but had cleverly advised them to ask their class teacher, the students picked up where Carrot left off.

'Isn't it exciting, sir?' asked Mathew. 'My mouth's watering. An actual convict!'

'Sir, do you think the escaped prisoner will come to our school?' Meena's eyes shone at the prospect.

'Why was he in prison, sir?' asked Mohan. 'Was he a murderer or a kidnapper? Or a smuggler?'

'How do I know all this?' Mr Prasad snapped. 'And how can he come here? We have a watchman and the gates are always closed. We are safe. Now open your books.'

'All are dead. Count the bodies!' screamed Carrot.

'This is too much!' Mr Prasad, already nervous, banged his book down. 'Remu, send Her Royal Highness out.'

Remu put her on the windowsill, and quick as lightning, the school cat jumped in. Carrot squawked in fright and sought refuge behind the blackboard. At that moment a sinister-looking man slunk quietly into the room, took a gun out of his pocket and, holding it against Mr Prasad's temple, snarled, 'Hands up! And all of you be quiet, or I'll shoot your teacher.'

The cat meowed loudly and shot out the way she had entered. Meena, now that her wish had come true, wailed. A few students began to cry while the rest sat frozen with terror.

'Come with me!' the man growled at Mr Prasad, who looked ashen.

'I have you covered! Hands up!' said a stern, official-sounding voice.

The man gave a start and looked around. 'Put down the gun, you rotten murderer. Shoot, everybody! Bang, bang, bang!' the voice continued. The hand holding the gun shook and something flew at the man's face. It was Carrot. She bit his ear. With a howl, he pushed her away and aimed the gun at her.

'Drop it or I'll blow your head off!' a grating voice came from the blackboard.

'Get him!' a stern voice boomed from a desk.

'We're all around you!' the ceiling now spoke.

The flummoxed convict turned his head in all directions in fear, and the gun fell from his limp hand to the floor. Quick as lightning, Remu snatched it away. The others, showing great presence of mind, now left their seats and, leaping forward, overpowered the man. Some sat on him while Carrot began screeching at the top of her voice. Hearing the fracas, the teachers from the nearby classrooms and the gardener rushed into the room. The grown-ups now took over. The convict was taken away and soon peace returned to the classroom.

Everyone fussed over Mr Prasad, who couldn't stop trembling. 'Thank you, Your Royal Highness!' he whispered to Carrot.

She said softly, 'Good boy! Swallow some gunpowder.'

'But what were those other voices? The room had people talking from everywhere.' Mr Prasad looked bewildered.

'Yes, how did that happen?' Meena was puzzled. 'It wasn't Carrot.'

'Well, that was me trying my ventriloquism,' Rajesh confessed, looking very pleased.

'Wow, Rajesh, that was a great performance!' The students crowded around this new hero, who basked in their admiration. 'How did you manage it?'

'I had been practising hard at home and wanted to give you a surprise before the final day of vacation classes,' Rajesh, who couldn't stop grinning, explained.

'You certainly did that!' said Mr Prasad, patting him on the back.

Carrot, not pleased that the fussing from everybody present had shifted to Rajesh, screamed, 'Don't utter a word! I'll have you kidnapped!'

'Oh, Carrot, Your Royal Highness, I'll miss you!' exclaimed Mr Prasad with a laugh as the children, realizing the parrot didn't take kindly to being ignored, began to shower her once again with praise and endearments.

'No more vacation classes!' Mrs Susy Joseph's voice seemed to come from the cupboard.

'Funny man!' Carrot cackled and flew to Rajesh's shoulder. 'Have a nut.'

At that moment, the intercom once again came to life, this time with a screech that would have done Carrot proud. Mrs Joseph's voice came floating out. 'Teachers and students, your attention please.'

Everyone turned to Rajesh, but he shook his head.

'Not guilty!' said Carrot, in a rough voice. 'But arrest him.'

Mrs Joseph's voice went on, 'The vacation classes were a success, but we have decided not to extend them. Tomorrow will be the last day.'

'Yaaaaaaaaaay!' The students almost blew off the ceiling with a jubilant yell.

Mr Prasad announced he would be giving the whole class a treat the next day, since it was Remu's last day at SAP.

'I'll miss Carrot,' he said to the parrot, holding out a finger. 'Come, Your Royal Highness!' he said rather bravely.

'Don't be a fool!' Carrot gave his finger a solid peck.

'Ooh!' Mr Prasad glared at her and withdrew his hand in pain.

'Hands up!' Carrot cackled.

**15 May**
**10.01 a.m.**

Dear Diary,

Yesterday was the first day of my summer vacation. Travelled by train to Usha Maushi's house with Baba. Baba went back. Amma is not well and needs him, he said.

Had dinner and went to sleep.

Ashwin

**16 May**
**10.07 a.m.**

Dear Diary,

Read all day yesterday. Watched some TV with Usha Maushi.

Ashwin

**17 May**
**2.39 p.m.**

Dear Diary,

Finished reading half the books I brought with me. Usha Maushi watches serials in which everyone cries. She tells us to go out. But there is nothing to do outside.

Ashwin

**18 May**
**9.14 a.m.**

Dear Diary,

This is the most boring summer vacation anyone ever spent! So bored that I am writing in my diary now, after eating breakfast, instead of at night. How Tanya Miss will laugh when she reads this!

I am stuck in this dark, musty house with Usha Maushi and my sister, Asha. My sister won't even let me sleep in peace! Last night she was scratching the wall between our rooms! Drove me mad. Finally, I banged on the wall with a fat vase. Maybe I banged too hard because a hole appeared in the wall and powdery white stuff rained down. Would the wall collapse? I couldn't sleep for worrying. But the wall is fine. The vase, though, has a dimple in it.

What if Usha Maushi sees it? (My third worry. Second worry is wall collapsing.) She might send us away. And we have no place to go. (Fourth and fifth worries!) Amma is in the hospital, Baba is taking care of her and none of our other relatives want us. We quarrel too much, they say—Asha and I. But Asha always starts it, like she began kicking me under the table today. I asked her to stop and she shouted at me for banging on the wall. So I shouted at her for scratching the wall. There was a lot of shouting. It's a good thing Usha Maushi is almost deaf. Otherwise we would have been sent home on the next train. ~~Silly~~ Asha!
*Lovely*

Ashwin

**19 May**
**9.41 a.m.**

Dear Diary,

I have the ~~nastiest,~~ ~~ugliest,~~ ~~meanest~~ older sister in
the world! She sneaked into my room, found this
diary and changed what I wrote about her yesterday.

*nicest prettiest kindest*

Here's the truth about Asha:

Asha is a ~~monster~~. She ~~hates~~ me. She has ~~hated~~
me from the moment I was born. She ~~always~~ fights
with me.

*fairy* *loves* *loved*

*never*

Other truths about Asha:

She's a fussy eater. Only crustless bread. Alu-
sabji without onions. Bhindi only if it's fried crisp
and black. She's the reason no one wants us to visit
them. Otherwise for summer vacation we could've
visited Manu Kaka in Shimla. Or Priti Maushi in
Goa. Instead, we are stuck in this old house because
Usha Maushi agreed to let us visit. Usha Maushi
can't hear well, so perhaps she hasn't heard all the
stories about us. She's a horrible cook. Lumpy rice,
hard rotis and she boils all the vegetables, even

cabbage! Huge green chillies in everything, even the yoghurt. Breakfast is stale brown bread, with sharp crusts that cut my tongue. You should see Asha's face at mealtimes. That's the best thing about this horrible summer vacation!

Thank you, Tanya Miss, for giving us holiday homework and asking us to keep a diary. Otherwise I might have forgotten these horrible details. Now I'll just read my summer diary to remember what happened in the vacation.

Ashwin*i*

**20 May**
**7.13 p.m.**

Dear Diary,

How is my ~~horrible~~ *wonderful* sister doing this? When did she sneak into my room? How did she find my diary? Especially after I found a really secret and safe place for it. Maybe she's a burglar because she found my diary, read it, even wrote in it! She changed my name from Ashwin to Ashwini! She does that to irritate me.

I am waiting to grow up so I can change my name. I will have a name so perfect it can't be changed, and I won't be teased about it. It will be my name, from start to finish, and no one, not even my ~~evil~~ *angelic* sister, Asha, will be able to change it!

How could I let my ~~wicked~~ *kind* sister get away this time? I had to tell her she was a ~~hateful~~ *loving* person for reading my diary.

But Asha seemed to have disappeared. She's so good at hiding that she should be a spy. She wasn't in her room or the living room. The kitchen was full of thick clouds and a horrible smell. Usha Maushi was drifting through the clouds, humming tunelessly as she created another ~~awful~~ *delicious* meal for us. It was like a scene from a horror movie. Suddenly my head was full of thoughts of ghosts. (My sixth worry!) A shiver ran down my spine and my ears filled with the heavy thudding of my heart. I tried to think happy thoughts of cake and ice cream and Diwali, but it was no use! Everywhere I looked I saw horrible shapes floating whitely about. I backed out of the kitchen, my legs shivering. Lights, I thought, lights would scare any ghosts away. But Usha Maushi only has dim yellow bulbs, and those leave miles and miles of darkness for ghosts to hide in.

So I walked very fast, looking for my sister. I peeped in at a door and saw a little terrace, full of shadows. A shadow moved suddenly and spoke my name. How my heart leapt in my chest! I nearly screamed! My brain was saying, 'Run, run, run!' But my legs, they seemed to have grown roots into the ground and simply wouldn't move. Someone spoke my name again, and then I saw that it was only my sister. Phew! I could finally breathe! My sister is so good at sitting still that she could be a statue. Then I asked her about my diary and she stopped being a statue. She leapt to her feet and danced about. She said she knew nothing of my diary and had better things to do than read it. And anyway, she said, she simply wasn't interested in my boring life.

I wanted to say many things to my ~~rude~~ *polite* sister. But Usha Maushi came to find us. I don't like fighting in front of people, so I said nothing at all. But I'll find a safer place for my diary. I'll lock it away. Asha can't open a lock!

Can she?

Ashwini

**21 May**
**10.02 a.m.**

Dear Diary,

So sleepy. But I am still writing. Because Tanya Miss is going to check every page of every diary. Asha found my diary again. And she wrote in it again. But how?

I am too sleepy to wonder.

I am too sleepy to even fight my sister.

Haven't slept at all. I got into bed last night and fell asleep. But I woke up because Asha was calling my name. My proper name, not the one she uses to tease me. I jumped out of bed and ran. (Didn't even worry about the dark.) What was wrong with my sister?

I thumped on her door, my heart thumping too. The minute Asha opened the door I knew that she was fine because she began shouting and calling me names. She said I was a ~~stupid~~ good boy, that I did ~~not~~ care for others and was ∧not selfish. I called her a few names too. Right in the middle of our shouting, there was another loud noise. A gust of wind had slammed our doors shut. Even that didn't stop us. My sister simply shouted louder. She should be an announcer, the kind that shouts at exhibitions and fairs. She wouldn't even need a microphone!

I wanted to sleep but my door wouldn't open. It was stuck. Then Asha took a break from all the shouting to laugh at me. But when she tried to open her door, that was stuck too!

We kicked our doors. We shouted at them. Our feet hurt, and our throats, but the doors stayed shut. Perhaps Usha Maushi could have helped? But she was fast asleep. What if she sent us home for disturbing her? Or told the other relatives about us? So we walked to the small terrace that Asha had found. There was a nice breeze and the moon was shining. We stood for some time, ignoring each other. Then we sat down. It was very peaceful. I was thinking of my Worry Number One. And suddenly Asha asked about Amma. What if she never came home from the hospital? For a minute I couldn't even speak, I was so shocked. How did my sister know that Amma's illness was my Worry Number One and that I was thinking about it?

Asha had many scary questions about Amma's illness. Discussing them didn't make my worry smaller. And it was still my Worry Number One. But it was nice to know that it was Asha's Worry Number One too. Then we tried to open our doors and they opened at once. What a mystery! But we were too tired to try to solve it. Instead, we fell asleep.

We were both sleepy this morning, but we became alert when we saw what Usha Maushi had made for breakfast. Puris and alu-sabji! Even my fussy sister loves puris. But the sabji had big chunks of onion in it. Asha looked so sad that I plucked all the onions from her plate and crunched them up. I did it even though my sister had found my diary again. And she'd called me Ashwini! Again!

Ashwini

**22 May**
**11.03 a.m.**

Dear Diary,

So I helped my sister by eating the onions from her sabji. And what did she do? She found my diary and she changed my name. It's like she can't stop being mean to me. But I could stop her fooling me again. I decided that I was not going to rescue Asha even if she screamed all night.

That was my plan. But the screams last night were not Asha's. They were mine. Asha came running as if the house were on fire, shouting, 'What, what, what?' I opened my eyes and pointed. There was a lizard, and it was right over my bed! (Lizards—Worry Number Eight. Or Nine.) A tiny smile appeared on her face. Then she swallowed the smile and chased the lizard out of the room.

There was nothing to say. So I said nothing.

But that night I slept well knowing no lizard was going to fall on me.

Ashwin

**23 May**
**7.41 a.m.**

Dear Diary,

It's difficult to shout at someone who has rescued you from a lizard. And it's impossible to fight with someone who has chased a lizard out of your room. So I didn't. But I was still not going to get fooled by any screams. That's what I thought when I went to bed yesterday.

I had only been asleep a few minutes when I heard someone call my name. *Hah*, I thought, and stuffed my fingers into my ears. But it was a difficult voice to ignore. And I realized that it was Usha Maushi calling for me and Asha. What could I do? I leapt out of bed and ran. I stopped to stick my suitcase in the doorway so the wind wouldn't slam it shut again. The voice was coming from the little terrace. Had Usha Maushi fallen down? But when I burst into the terrace I only saw Asha.

My sister had fooled me again! She could be an actress because she can imitate voices. I called her a ~~silly~~ *good* girl. She called me a ~~foolish~~ *smart* boy. And then

147

a gust of wind slammed the terrace door shut. Of course, it was jammed, but this time we knew what to do. We sat in silence till one of us said something, and then, it was like a lock had clicked open. So we began talking.

We talked about Amma, who was getting better, and Usha Maushi's cooking. Asha said we should help her cook. I thought she was joking, but no! My sister is often filled with kind and helpful thoughts about others, and it turned out that she had made plans for how we could help Usha Maushi. We were so busy discussing these that we didn't even notice when the terrace door swung open. When we went to bed, I felt very silly when I saw my suitcase standing in the door like a guard, but Asha said it was a brilliant idea.

Asha, calling me brilliant! I was smiling when I fell asleep.

Ashwin

**24 May**
**8.01 a.m.**

Dear Diary,

Change in breakfast menu! No brown bread. Only fluffy pancakes made by my sister. My sister could be a chef, she cooks so well. Usha Maushi loved the pancakes. She sat down groaning and moaning, and ate four. And I realized that I had never seen Usha Maushi sit down and eat. At mealtimes she's always walking between the kitchen and the dining room, carrying food. Kind thoughts filled me, but before I could say anything Asha offered to cook lunch. Asha and I could have been twins, we share so many thoughts.

We joked with each other as we shopped for Usha Maushi and later made khichdi for lunch. Asha made raita too. Raita is difficult because Asha doesn't eat yoghurt. Instead, she makes it with lemon juice and other things. My sister could be an inventor and invent recipes!

Ashwin

**25 May**
**11.46 a.m.**

Dear Diary,

Went to the zoo with Usha Maushi yesterday.
Sandwiches and cake made by me and Asha. Usha
Maushi ate three pieces of cake. I ate five!

Ashwin

**26 May**
**9.57 a.m.**

Dear Diary,

Went to a fair with Usha Maushi. I ate cotton
candy and popcorn. Usha Maushi and I had a
competition to see who could eat more pani puris.
She won. She ate so many pani puris that Asha and
I thought she would burst. But she let out a huge
burp and was fine. On the giant wheel my tummy
began to feel funny. Usha Maushi was in another

carriage and she kept shouting instructions to us. But Asha didn't need any instructions—she knew how to make me feel better. My sister could be a nurse because she knows how to take care of people who are sick.

But I think I won't eat so many pani puris again.

It's not a good idea.


Ashwin


**27 May**
**9.06 a.m.**

Dear Diary,


Usha Maushi took us boating on a lake yesterday. We carried a picnic lunch and came back tired.


Ashwin
But we had a lot of fun.

**28 May**
**8.09 a.m.**

Dear Diary,

Usha Maushi wants to invite her friends to tea. And she wants me and Asha to help her cook! Can we do it? My sister says we can!

Ashwin

**29 May**
**7.39 a.m.**

Dear Diary,

Baking all day. And cleaning the house. Tired!

Ashwin

**30 May**
**9.23 a.m.**

Dear Diary,

Someone rang the doorbell yesterday morning, and when we opened the door it was Baba. For a minute

Asha and I were thinking of the same thing—our Worry Number One. We could be twins because we are so alike. But Baba had come to take us home because Amma is better. Soon she'll be back with us!

Of course, we were happy about that. But Asha and I became sad and quiet when we thought of leaving Usha Maushi's house so soon. And Usha Maushi? She became very loud and began to argue with Baba. She didn't want him to take us away. Baba couldn't believe his ears. Neither could Asha and I. Usha Maushi said we had been promised to her for a month (as if we were some kind of nice gift!), we were the best guests she had ever had and that she wanted us to stay longer. Baba kept looking at us to see if we were the same Ashwin and Asha.

What do you do when someone says nice things about you? We didn't know, because people don't usually say nice things about us. So we stood like statues, but inside we were smiling and smiling. Then Usha Maushi fed Baba our cake, praised our cooking and, finally, Baba smiled and let us stay.

We had a party that evening on the little terrace with puris and alu-sabji without onions and ice cream.

The breeze blew and we spoke in quiet voices. It was wonderfully peaceful, and there were many things to make us happy. It was wonderful that Usha Maushi actually wanted us to stay with her. And even more wonderful that Worry Number One was gone and Amma was out of danger. Of course, Asha was as happy as I was, and that's why I dared to ask her about my diary.

There were so many things I wanted to know.

Like how exactly had Asha found my diary? And when had she managed to read it and change my words?

Asha stared at me and said she didn't know I had a diary, and she had never read or written in it.

Then it was my turn to stare at her. Someone had found my diary. And that someone had written in it. If it was not Asha, who was it?

I could feel my heart thump in excitement. This was a mystery, the first real mystery of my life, and I was excited and scared and worried all at once. But I was determined about one thing—this mystery had to be solved. And the only person who could help me solve it was my sister, Asha.

So I showed her my diary. It was only when I handed it to her that I remembered that the diary was full of all the bad names I had called her. Anyone would get upset reading those things about themselves. But my sister is not like anyone. She laughed when she read my diary. And then she said I wrote very well. And that I should become a writer!

Ashwin

**31 May**
**4.41 p.m.**
Dear Diary,

Baba left. Things are back to normal. We are preparing for Usha Maushi's party. The house looks clean and fresh. The kitchen is full of lovely smells. The terrace has flower pots and twinkling lights, tables for the food and comfortable chairs.

It is difficult to do this kind of work in silence. Asha and I talked and discussed and wondered about many things. Ever since I showed Asha my diary, we have come up with various theories about who could have written in it. For a little while we were sure Usha Maushi had done it. Then Asha asked Usha Maushi to write something so we could compare her handwriting with the one in my diary. But the two writings did not match, so we had to think again.

And once we began to think, we realized that several strange things had happened. I remembered the scratching on my wall and Asha remembered the slamming doors. And both of us realized that not one door had slammed or jammed in the past few days. And from somewhere in our discussion came one word—ghosts! (Worry Number Six.) I don't know who said it first, but it scared us both. Asha's eyes got all big and shiny, and as for me, my heart was jumping so hard I could barely speak. My mouth was suddenly dry, and I had to swallow before I could say anything. And when we could finally speak, both of us were full of questions that we threw at each other. Neither of us knew the answers to any of them, and that only made us feel even more scared.

We both agreed that the answers to our questions would have made us feel so much better. *Really?*

Had there really been a ghost wandering about the house? *Yes.*

Was it an evil ghost? *NO.*

Perhaps, I said, it had left now that its work was done. *Ha ha! NO.*

Asha said we had to be grateful to the ghost because it had helped us both so much. *Oh ... yes!*

But when I remembered how it had tricked me, I wasn't so sure. *Just you wait!*

The questions kept us talking to each other, making guesses and laughing at each other's suggestions. And that, we realized, was all that mattered. *You are so right!*

Ashwini

*Excellent work, Ashwin! Enjoyed reading about your summer.*

*Did you really feel better once you had the answers to your questions? The answers sound far more worrying than your questions!*

*When are you going back to Usha Maushi's house? Soon, I hope, because I will be waiting to read your diary. Yes, that means you will be writing a vacation diary. Again.*

*T. Verma*

# TUMBURU'S VACATION

Prashant Pinge

Tumburu was delighted. His holiday pass had just arrived. After 453 years of pushing paper in Svarga Loka's Akashik Records department, the *gandharva*'s vacation request had finally been granted.

'You must visit Mahar Loka,' Cittasena said, closing the ledger. 'It's beautiful this time of the year.'

Panada looked over from his cubicle. 'That's where you go to meditate with the rishis,' he smirked. 'But if you want to have fun, Bhuvar Loka should be your destination. They've recently got a new theme park with a killer Surya Samrat ride.'

'I'm thinking of Prithvi Loka,' Tumburu declared.

'Pri . . . Prithvi Loka?' Panada gulped, glancing around to see whether anybody else had heard. He continued in hushed tones, 'You're not serious, are you? It's a barbaric place, I'm told.'

'After spending centuries behind this desk, I'm looking for some real adventure.'

'Then visit Pataal Loka,' Cittasena said, retrieving the quill he had dropped. 'Vasuki, the Naga king, has recently removed gandharvas from the no-fly list.'

'Have you forgotten about Nala?' Panada chimed in. 'He had to be institutionalized after his visit to Prithvi Loka. Why do you think no one has visited the place in over two centuries?'

'And what about Vishnu himself? He hasn't stepped back on Prithvi Loka after his Krishna avatar.'

'Exactly! Even the devas fled from this place eons ago.'

'Indra and the other devas have gone soft,' Tumburu retorted. 'All they do is drink soma and dance with the apsaras. Besides, I'm only going to be on Prithvi Loka from dusk till dawn. What could possibly go wrong in twelve hours?'

'This is beautiful,' Tumburu said with a sigh the moment he had materialized on Prithvi Loka.

While his vision was still blurred, courtesy of the ether through which he had journeyed, Tumburu could make out the gentle curves of the rolling hills that traversed the vast green expanse. He could also see the outline of some *manavas* who seemed to be waving to him. *What a friendly lot!* he thought.

Alas, it was only an illusion. As it so happened, Tumburu soon realized that he was standing in front of a large hoarding that was advertising an upcoming township with a happy family and all.

Unfortunately, it was also the exact instant in which his ears popped, suddenly filling his auditory passages with a cacophony of sounds. The noises were even worse than what he had experienced while travelling through Rasatal Loka, which was infested with unruly *danavas*. And those guys really knew how to create a din!

But Tumburu was in for an even bigger shock when he turned around. Instead of the picture he had conjured up in his mind, he was treated to a sea of manavas bustling along pavements in the midst of what could only be described as a concrete jungle. Worse still, there were metal monsters zooming up and down the roads, honking and screeching for no apparent reason.

Tumburu froze. For, you see, while he had judiciously avoided Panipat, the location where Nala, his predecessor, had landed at the inopportune time when the Marathas were engaged in a fierce battle with the Afghans, he had managed to insert himself at a road intersection in Dadar, one of Mumbai's most crowded suburbs, at the busiest time of the day.

After momentary panic, Tumburu decided that the most prudent course of action would be to take a deep breath. While it did send him into an incessant coughing fit, it also broke the spell of fear that had overwhelmed him. After all, he thought as he rubbed his aching ribs, it was he who had sought adventure. And the only way he could have one was to immerse himself into everything that Prithvi Loka had to offer. With that, Tumburu stepped onto the road.

A metal monster came charging at him before braking and swerving around him at the last moment. Now, gandharvas pride themselves on being hardy creatures. But Tumburu had no illusions about the kind of damage the monster could have inflicted on him. As if that wasn't enough, he also had to suffer through a volley of verbal abuses hurled at him by the manava driving the monster.

Just then the signal turned red, and the metal monsters came to a hasty halt. Tumburu had yet to recover from his ordeal, but that wasn't going to stop the restless Mumbai crowd from crossing the road. And just like that, the gandharva found himself riding the crest of the wave, battling impatient nudges and sharp elbows. Before long, he had been deposited on the other side, bruised but still in one piece.

Tumburu managed to soothe his frayed nerves. And promptly fell into a ditch.

For the briefest of moments, Tumburu felt like he was descending into Naraka itself. After all, with how things had gone so far, it wasn't that far-fetched to think that Prithvi Loka had a direct passageway leading straight to hell. As it so happened, it was a shallow hole conveniently forgotten by the municipality, and the gandharva managed to scramble out with his dignity intact.

But there was another dilemma awaiting his ascent. Wherever he looked, all he could see were manavas. The place was infested with these creatures. No wonder there was a crisis brewing in the seven netherworlds. After all, where could they accommodate so many souls?

Tumburu's train of thought, however, was interrupted by an interesting phenomenon. The manavas around him seemed to be in intense discussions with their fellow beings, which seemed to have a pattern that went something like this:

'I shall give you so many rupees.'

'No, I can reduce the price by only so many rupees.'

'This is my final offer.'

'I cannot go below this price.'

Tumburu was, in fact, witnessing the classic manava art of haggling. He did remember stories about how the devas had engaged in a similar activity with the asuras in their desire to gain control of amrit, the nectar of immortality. But there had been a lot at stake. On Prithvi Loka, it seemed to be a way of life. How utterly vile!

The gandharva, however, couldn't help but chuckle when he saw a vendor selling posters of his masters. The manavas did have rather wild imaginations. But where was Indra? The king of the devas would not be pleased.

By the time Tumburu had reached the end of Dadar's market, a cloak of darkness had fallen over the area. The shops that ran alongside, quite subdued till then, were now brightly lit. The roads were also illuminated by yellow beams. A few nervous minutes later, he had navigated the road without any incident. The gandharvas had been careful to keep his elbows handy this time around.

'Which drama are you acting in?' a thin manava shouted from the shadows of a tiny tea stall.

'A cheap production of the Mahabharata?' his stocky friend offered, amidst snickers from all around.

In that moment, it dawned upon Tumburu that he wasn't dressed appropriately for Prithvi Loka. In all fairness, it wasn't his fault. After all, his only reference point had been the fractured account from Nala that had been recorded over two centuries ago. The gandharva looked down in despair at his chunky jewellery and embroidered red shawl with colourful beads, pearls and other stones that he had donned above the crisp purple dhoti flowing below.

At least he had heeded Cittasena's advice and left his crown behind.

There had been plenty of comments from passers-by earlier, but they had all been drowned in the chaos surrounding Tumburu's own travails. The residential section of Dadar, however, was quieter.

'I'm sure he plays a rakshasa,' another manava interjected cheekily. 'Just check out that nose ring.'

'Look, he's even striking a pose,' the first manava guffawed as the others burst into laughter.

In reality, a very riled-up Tumburu had been prepared to strike them down with a *parivartaka* mantra, a spell that would turn them into dung. It didn't work, of course. After all, Rule 218, Subsection 14.5 of the etiquette guidelines clearly stated that the lower Svarga Loka beings couldn't use magic in Prithvi Loka.

A disillusioned Tumburu wandered down the path, suddenly conscious of his attire. He was about to slink into a dark patch cast by one of the trees when his eyes fell upon a park. It was along the periphery of a large field that seemed to be some sort of recreational gathering area for the manavas.

The sight of Shivaji Park served to rev up his sagging spirits, and the gandharva decided to proceed to the oasis for a much-needed meditative break.

Tumburu, however, would only make it as far as the frankie stall. For, you see, Gogo, a rather mangy-looking mongrel with a chewed-out ear, had come up empty-handed after scouring through paper wrappers for mutton scraps that very moment. And he decided to take out his frustration by vowing to separate the gandharva from his flapping dhoti.

Tumburu, who was feeling a sense of kinship with any species other than the manavas, made the cardinal mistake of stopping to flash a genial smile at the canine.

*How dare this funny-smelling creature mock me*, Gogo thought, baring his fangs. The very next moment, he made a beeline for the gandharva's heels.

Tumburu was caught completely unawares by this unprovoked display of hostility. However, it took him but a fraction of a second to gather up his dhoti and take a detour into one of the by-lanes. That marked the end of his rejuvenation plans in Shivaji Park.

While the chase had been initiated by Gogo, he had soon been joined by a few of his stray brethren. Tumburu, who had spent most of his waking life behind a desk, suddenly began to discover muscles in his legs that he never knew existed. Having finally determined that he couldn't outrun the canine brigade, the gandharva somehow managed to scramble on top of a red metal monster parked on the side of the road.

While most of the other dogs had abandoned the pursuit before long, Gogo showed an admirable resolve to fulfil his vow. However, a shower of eggs from one of the upper floors of a neighbouring building broke his resolve. He glared at the gandharva and ducked out of the lane.

Tumburu was about to join his hands in a show of gratitude when an egg shot at him like a missile and caught him squarely on the chest. Well, that was the end of that. He stumbled down the side and ran the other way until he was out of the assailant's range.

The lane curved through the neighbourhood until it reached the main road. Tumburu spotted the periphery of the opposite side of Shivaji Park. But there was a pressing matter that needed immediate attending to. He was covered in egg splatter. And he was not only sticky but also stinking.

As if on cue, the July skies opened up, and it started pouring. Tumburu's head went limp. Indra was having the last laugh after all.

A few minutes later, a broken Tumburu found himself taking shelter under the canopy of a tree. His trip to Prithvi Loka had been a disaster so far. For the first time since he had landed, the gandharva found himself yearning for the familiarity of Svarga Loka. But the stars told him he still had about seven hours before he could get back home.

'I like your clothes,' a tiny voice suddenly piped up from his side. 'What's your name?'

Tumburu glanced down. It was a little girl, perhaps eight, with dishevelled hair. She was wearing a worn-out dress in a floral print.

'Tumburu.'

'That's a funny name. I'm Chitra.'

'I know an apsara called Chitra.'

The little girl shrugged. 'I'm the only Chitra I know.'

Tumburu smiled. Suddenly, he didn't feel all that alone. But before he could say anything, Chitra was ready with her next question.

'Where are you from?' she asked.

'From Svarga Loka,' he replied, pointing to the skies.

'For real?'

Before the gandharva could offer a nod, his stomach gave a loud growl.

'Would you like to eat vada pav?'

Tumburu looked confused. The only foods available in Svarga Loka were soma and amrita.

'You must try it.' Chitra caught his hand and dragged him across the road.

They soon reached a cart parked under a tree. It was illuminated by a dim bulb hanging from one of the lower branches. As expected, Tumburu was getting stares. But he didn't care. The smell of the sizzling vadas had captivated his senses.

'My mouth is on fire, but I can't stop eating,' Tumburu said, chomping away on the vada pav. 'It's so tasty.'

'Isn't it?' Chitra mumbled back. 'But we're not done yet. You must try the bhajis as well.'

The gandharva bobbed his head. He had been eyeing them for some time. Moments later, he was tucking away into the oval potato patties. A blob of chutney dripped on to his dhoti, but he ignored it.

'And now,' Chitra said, beckoning to a turbaned manava on a cycle nearby, 'it's time for something sweet.'

They were soon slurping down pink strawberry kulfis. Tumburu refused to talk until he had licked the stick clean. 'This is the best meal I've ever had,' he said with sigh, rubbing his stomach contentedly.

'Do you want to have more fun?' Chitra asked.

Tumburu had been about to slump in the bent metal chair but straightened up immediately. The spark of adventure that had brought him all the way to Prithvi Loka had been ignited once again.

'Then let's go,' Chitra cried, looping her arm through his and guiding him diagonally across to the end of the road.

'But the garden is closed,' he said, noticing the thick padlock hanging between the chains.

Chitra winked at him. 'Not for us,' she said with a grin, parting some of the thick foliage that had grown over the fence in the corner. There was a gap just wide enough for them to squeeze through.

Tumburu could see beautifully landscaped patches of green intersected by cobbled paths that ran through like the veins on a leaf. The silhouettes of tall trees loomed above while droplets of water holding on to the blades of grass gleamed under the moon's warm light. The only sounds they could hear were the lashing of the waves beyond and the muted hum of the metal monsters from the road on the other side. A cool breeze meandered from the open seas, filling Tumburu's heart with a sense of peace.

'So why did you come here all the way from Svarga Loka?' Chitra asked, sitting on the steps of the large pergola in the centre of the park.

'Do you really want to know?' Tumburu asked, resting against one of the pillars.

She nodded eagerly.

'I'm a gandharva,' he disclosed, sighing and looking away wistfully. 'Traditionally, we were musicians and warriors. But over time, things changed. The devas made peace with the asuras. Then they lost interest in Prithvi Loka. But someone had to shoulder the responsibility. And that fell upon the gandharvas. I just couldn't take the boring life any longer.'

'So are you having fun?'

Tumburu shook his head vehemently. 'I've almost been run over by a metal monster, fallen into a hole, teased by some hooligans, chased by a four-legged creature and been drenched to the bone.'

'You're like my father,' Chitra said thoughtfully. 'He wasn't happy when he had a job. And then he lost his job. But he still isn't happy.'

Tumburu didn't reply immediately. 'I still can't help but wish I had gone to Bhuvar Loka. I was told it has a new theme park. And Indra only knows when I can get my next holiday pass.'

'Is that all?' Chitra said, rolling her eyes. She pointed to a corner of the park that was filled with dark silhouettes of different shapes and sizes. 'We have one right here.'

Much to Tumburu's astonishment, he found himself in front of a vast array of recreational apparatus. And so, they zipped back and forth on swings, whizzed down slides without a care, sped around in circles on wooden horses, bobbed up and down on the see-saw, sprayed each other with sand and burrowed their way through colourful tunnels. It was only after a couple of hours of intense fun that they fell back on to the grass, exhausted.

'That was something,' Tumburu gasped. When he opened his eyes, he found himself staring at the infinite black firmament dotted with sparkling white stars.

'It really was.'

'Can I ask you something?'

'Sure.'

'Why aren't you troubled like the other manavas?'

Chitra thought for a moment. 'Because I want to enjoy every moment.'

Neither of them said anything for a few minutes.

'Tumburu, can you please sing a song for me?'

'I would be delighted to.'

The gandharva cleared his throat and began his celestial song. His voice reverberated through the silent night, filled with the sweetness of amrita. He sang about heroic battles and lost kingdoms, great sacrifices and treacherous acts, eternal love and broken promises. His songs rose to greet the heavens and fell to plead for forgiveness. Tears streamed down Tumburu's cheeks, but he continued to sing.

'. . . suddenly, I heard a tiny snore,' Tumburu continued, smiling.

'And then?' Cittasena asked, almost on the edge of his seat.

'Well, it was almost dawn. So I left her my necklace as a gift. As the first rays of the sun broke through, I could feel my being merge with the ether, and I was whisked away back to Svarga Loka.'

Panada drew in his breath. 'That was quite an adventure.'

'So are you happy you chose Prithvi Loka?' Cittasena asked.

Tumburu shrugged, recalling his little friend's words. 'The only thing that matters is this moment.'

'This is unfair!' the boys complained. 'We refuse to be taught by a new pundit.'

The new punditmoshai they were expecting was named Kalikumar Tarkalankar.

After the holidays, the boys were returning to school by train from their respective homes. One of them, a witty fellow, had composed a poem about the new pundit, called 'Kalo Kumror Balidan' (the sacrificial death of the black pumpkin), which all of them were reciting at the top of their voices. Just then, an old gentleman boarded the train at Arkhol station. With him he carried his *kantha*-wrapped bedding roll, two or three earthen handis sealed with rags, a tin trunk and a few bundles. A tough-looking boy, known to everyone as Bichkun, called out: 'There's no room for you here, old man. Go find another carriage.'

'It's too crowded,' the old man replied. 'There's no room anywhere. I'll just take this little corner; I won't bother you at all.' With these words, he left the bench to them and moved to a corner of the floor, where he spread out his bedding.

'Baba,' he asked the boys, 'where are you all going, and for what purpose?'

'To perform a *sraddha*,' Bichkun declared. 'A funeral ceremony.'

'Whose sraddha is it?' the old man enquired.

'Kalo-Kumro-Tatka-Lanka's' was the reply.

The boys chorused in a loud, sing-song chant:

'*Kalo-Kumro-Tatka-Lanka, black-pumpkin-green-chilli,*
*We'll teach you a lesson and make you look silly!*'

The train halted at Asansol. The old man got off to have a bath. As soon as he returned to the carriage afterwards, Bichkun warned him: 'Don't remain in this carriage, sir!'

'Why, may I ask?'

'It's infested with rats.'

'Rats! How's that possible?'

'Just look at the mess they made when they got into those handis of yours.'

The gentleman found that the handi full of sugary kodmas was now completely empty, and the one containing khoichur had not a grain left in it.

'And they even ran off with whatever was inside your rag bundle,' Bichkun added.

That bundle had contained four or five ripe mangoes from his garden.

'The rats are famished, I see,' remarked the gentleman with a faint smile.

'No, no, it's their nature to devour things even if they're not hungry,' replied Bichkun.

The boys laughed uproariously. 'Yes, moshai,' they guffawed, 'if there had been more, they'd have eaten it up as well.'

'I made a mistake,' the gentleman observed. 'Had I known there would be so many rats travelling together in the train, I would have carried some more stuff.'

The boys were disheartened to find that the old man did not lose his temper in spite of so much teasing. If he had been provoked, it would have been fun.

The train stopped at Burdwan. It would halt there for about an hour, to switch tracks.

'Baba,' said the gentleman, 'I won't trouble you any more. There will be room for me in another compartment.'

'No, no, that won't do. You must travel in the same coach as us. If there's anything left inside your bundles, we will guard it together, all of us. Nothing will be lost.'

'All right,' the gentleman assented. 'Get into the carriage, all of you. I'll join you in a little while.'

So the boys got into the carriage. A little later, the sweet seller's cart came and halted before their compartment, accompanied by the gentleman. Handing a paper bag to each of the boys, he said: 'Now there will be no shortage of food at the rats' feast.'

'Hurrah!' shouted the boys, jumping up in glee. The mango seller also arrived there, with his basket of mangoes.

There was no dearth of mangoes either, at their feast.

'Tell us,' the boys asked the gentleman, 'where are you going? What will you do there?'

'I am going in search of work,' he replied. 'I'll get off wherever I find work.'

They clapped their hands, all of them, and said: 'Come to our school then.'

'Why would your authorities want to keep me?'

'They must. We won't let Kalo-Kumro-Tatka-Lanka set foot in our neighbourhood.'

'You have put me in a difficult position, I must say! What if the secretary doesn't approve of me?'

'He must approve—or else we shall all leave the school.'

'All right, then take me with you.'

The train arrived at their station. The secretary was there in person. Seeing the old man, he cried: 'Welcome, welcome, Tarkalankar-moshai! Your house is ready and waiting.' With these words, he bowed at the old man's feet to offer his respects.

A version of this story first appeared in *The Land of Cards: Stories, Poems and Plays for Children*.

HOW I LOST
MY TONSILS
Manjula Padmanabhan

My tonsils got infected when I was eleven. At the time, my parents and I lived in Bangkok, the capital of Thailand. Three years later, in January 1967, my parents moved to Tehran, the capital of Iran. Instead of going with them, I went to a boarding school in Kodaikanal, which is in south India.

During all this time my tonsils were either infected, about to get infected or just getting over being infected. In case you're wondering, the tonsils are a pair of glands at the back of the throat. Most of us never notice them until they get infected. Then they swell up and look like two tiny red balloons in a place where no balloons should ever be.

During my first year at boarding school, my tonsils were inflamed—that is, infected—so regularly that I had a constant mild fever. I didn't mind too much, because it was very cold in Kodaikanal. While everyone else was shivering, I was toasty warm. But the back of my throat felt like it was coated with broken glass. Eating and drinking were painful.

My school was more like a military academy than a storybook school: very posh but also super strict. At 7500 feet, the climate was wet and misty most of the year. Wake-up was at 6.30 a.m. Morning assembly was at 7 a.m. Lights out at 9 p.m. Baths only twice a week because of water rationing.

There was no question of telling my parents that I'd rather be with them. I was pretty sure they would not agree. Sending me to boarding school had been a perfect solution, given their difficult travel schedule. So even though the three long years stretching ahead of me felt like a prison sentence, I was determined not to complain about anything. Including my throat.

Sometimes, in order to get relief, I would visit the infirmary. It was a little room by the side of the principal's office, in the school's main building. Rosy-cheeked Sister Christopher sat there in the evenings, examining girls who came to her with fevers, cuts and bruises.

She'd ask me to open my mouth. Whenever she peered inside, she'd jerk back in shock, muttering, 'Good gracious me, gerl!' in her Irish accent. 'Whar did yeh find THAT nasty thing?' She'd reach for a little bamboo stick with a wad of cotton wrapped around the end of it. She'd dip the wadded end into a pot of something dark red and faintly sweet. Grabbing my chin to hold my mouth open, she'd jab the back of my throat with the swab. The result was a vague but pleasing numbness.

Now and then a very weird thing would happen. A small hard lump would slide into my mouth from INSIDE MY THROAT.

The first time this happened, I was in my dorm, sitting up in bed under three blankets, waiting for the lights to be turned off. The white curtains that separated each of us sixteen girls from one another were drawn around my little space. No one could see me. So I spat the lump out on to my palm, feeling mildly horrified. I thought at first that one of my teeth had suddenly leapt off my gums and into my mouth. The object was smooth and ivory-white but the wrong shape to be a tooth. And anyway, none of my teeth were missing.

I stared at the strange object, wondering what to do with it. I'd never heard of such a thing happening to anyone. Should I be frightened or thrilled or— what? As a fourteen-year-old, I was also terrified of being labelled a weirdo. I didn't, for instance, want to be remembered for evermore as the Girl Who Spits Up Random Chunks of Ivory. I decided that my best bet was to just flush it down the toilet. I prayed that it wasn't some form of cancer, and I certainly hoped it would never happen again.

Needless to say, it DID happen again. Repeatedly. By the fourth time, I finally realized there was some connection between the white objects and the red balloons at the back of my throat. When the balloons reached maximum redness, the lumps would appear.

Then one day in the library, in a magazine for teenagers, I read an article about tonsillitis. That's the official name given to an inflammation of these glands. According to the article, infected tonsils release toxic chemicals that can seep into the brain, sometimes leading to a coma! And possibly even DEATH!

Looking back, I can see that the article had been written with a teenage audience in mind, presented with maximum drama. However, it mentioned the mysterious white objects that had been appearing in my mouth. They had a name: tonsilloliths. The word literally means 'tonsil stones'. They can form when the glands remain inflamed over long periods of time.

For me, reading the article was like hearing ten fire alarms going off at once. Clearly inaction was no longer an option! I was in the ninth standard. A mere two and a half years remained before the finals. In those days the exam was called the Senior Cambridge, because the papers were set and graded in England. I needed every last brain cell at my command if I wanted to pass my exams and leave school behind me forever. How could I possibly succeed if sitting right inside my throat was a pair of potential assassins otherwise known as Tonsil Left and Tonsil Right?

With my entire future at stake, I wrote to my parents, imploring them to arrange for the surgery when I visited them in Tehran that December. I must have made a very convincing case because a week later my mother wrote back to say she was sorry to hear about my difficulties and that yes, we would explore the snip-snip option during my winter hols.

I was SO delighted! I'd never had any surgery before, but I wasn't in the least scared. I knew, from countless children's books, that the one surgery every child can safely enjoy is a tonsillectomy. Why? Because after a brief nap in the surgical theatre, the prescribed treatment is ICE CREAM all day long for up to one week.

Even the article I had read in the magazine mentioned the ice cream diet. The reason it's the ideal food for recovery is that scooping flesh out of the back of the throat necessarily leaves two nasty bleeding holes behind. Eating normal food under these conditions is not just torture but can also prevent the wounds from healing. Ice cream cools and soothes the area, besides giving the patient something yummy to look forward to. No one mentioned the yummy bit to me, but it seemed only too obvious.

By the time I flew from Bombay's international airport to Tehran, I was thinking of the operation as an unusual but thrilling adventure: Sleep! Snip-snip! Ice cream! The sheer anticipation coloured my appreciation of Iran in bright delight. Everything about the country was superlative, from the moment of arrival. The avenues were broad, clean and tree-lined. The buildings were stately and well-proportioned. The people in the streets, both men and women, were startlingly beautiful. With their jet-black hair, creamy skin and heavy-lidded eyes rimmed with thick lashes, they all looked as if they had just stepped out of a classical painting.

Our home had six bedrooms and a gracious formal garden with a pair of willow trees bending over a pool. It was cold, of course, being the middle of December. When tiny snowflakes began drifting down out of the sky on my very first night, I felt all sparkly with happiness.

I wanted to get the operation over with as soon as possible, so I mentioned it at breakfast the next morning. I discovered, to my surprise, that my father did not approve of the procedure. 'Why take the risk?'

he wanted to know. 'Surgery is not a joke. Something can always go wrong. Best to avoid it unless absolutely necessary.'

I had no idea what he was talking about. None of the books I'd read had mentioned any kind of danger. A brief sleep followed by unlimited ice cream. What could go wrong?

'The tonsils are poisoning my brain!' I whined. 'I could fall into a coma and become a vegetable for the rest of my life!' I imagined myself as a giant cabbage, lolling mutely in bed.

My mother intervened. 'Let's go see the doctor,' she said. 'Then we'll decide.' So off we went, just me and Mum, to the 'Russian Hospital'.

It must have had some other name, but that's what we called it at the Indian embassy. The doctors were all Russian and spoke only Russian. The nurses were from the border areas between Iran and Russia, so they spoke both Russian and Farsi, the language of Iran. English, alas, was in short supply.

We had the embassy interpreter, Mr Ghosh, with us when we went to see Dr Alexis, the ENT surgeon. The doctor had grey eyes, curly brown hair and said he knew a few words of English. When I opened my mouth to display my tonsils his bushy eyebrows hit the ceiling. 'Whuf!' he said. Mr Ghosh said nothing because such words don't need translation. The surgery was scheduled for two days later.

The hospital was a huge place, with gleaming floors and pristine white walls. I was on the fourth floor, in a pleasant airy room all to myself. There seemed to be very few other patients. I was admitted the night before the surgery. We were all astonished to find that I needed an overnight stay. When Mr Ghosh expressed surprise, the attendant nurse told him it wouldn't be just one night but a whole week.

'But the operation will be over in five minutes!' exclaimed my mother.

The nurse explained to Mr Ghosh that I had bronchitis as a result of the inflamed tonsils. I might get seriously ill after the surgery. So it had to be a week. Both my parents came to settle me into my room for the night. My mother said she'd be back in the morning before the surgery. Dad still looked worried. Then they left. I had a book to read and my dinner that night was a hunk of hearty bread and borscht. It's made from beetroot and looks like dragon's blood—a rich, deep purple. It was delicious.

I was thrilled to find I could ask for Turkish coffee. In the three days I'd been in Iran I had already acquired a taste for this preparation, which looks and tastes like sweet, hot mud. In restaurants it's served in tiny gold cups at the end of a meal. When you drain the cup, someone comes over to read your fortune in the thick residue (called 'grounds') left behind. In the hospital, the cup was tiny but plain white, and there was no one to read the grounds. Even so, I enjoyed the very grown-up act of deciding I wanted something unusual, then getting it.

It was certainly strange that I'd be gone a whole week. But it was going to be ice cream all the way, so why worry? I wondered when I'd get to choose flavours. My favourite was (and still is) plain vanilla with hot chocolate sauce on the side. It was possible, however, that the hospital disapproved of chocolate sauce. I had hoped to ask one of the nurses in case any of them spoke English. When I discovered that they really didn't, I decided to ask Mr Ghosh about it when I saw him in the morning.

But my plans were derailed by an unfamiliar nurse who woke me up at 5 a.m. Since I couldn't understand her and Mr Ghosh wasn't present, we had to rely on sign language. She flipped her hand over a couple of times, from which I understood that she wanted me to lie face down on my bed. Then she gestured for me to pull down my pyjama bottoms. She gave me an injection of something that felt like liquid barbed wire travelling down my veins.

*Ow-ow-ow!* I thought, saying nothing out loud. There was no point protesting once the injection had been given. Still, the incident left me feeling uneasy. I wondered what else might happen over which I had no control.

I fell asleep once more, and when I next awoke, it was almost 7 o'clock. Mr Ghosh and my mum arrived. My bright airy room was suddenly bustling with nurses and bouquets of flowers that people from the embassy had sent. I saw that my mother was tense, and I knew it was because Dad still didn't approve. She was also annoyed with me for having got so sick in the first place. In her view, well-behaved children simply did not get sick.

In the midst of all this, I forgot to ask Mr Ghosh about the ice cream.

Then it was time to go. I waved goodbye to my mother as I walked out. 'Remember, I won't be able to talk when I get back!' I said. I knew from what I'd read that a carved-up throat is just as painful to talk with as to swallow with.

Mr Ghosh walked along with me, towards the swing doors of the theatre. He asked me if I was nervous. 'Not at all!' I replied. He was wise enough not to question my confidence.

When we reached the doors, the nurse who was with us told Mr Ghosh that he couldn't come any farther. This was a shock. I had just assumed he'd be with me all the way. As she led me through the doors to the other side, for the first time I felt a faint tremor of anxiety. Why couldn't he come with me? How would the doctor and nurses communicate with me? What if I needed something for which there were no obvious hand signals?

There was certainly no point asking the nurse, so I didn't try.

Without further discussion, she draped a floor-length plastic bib on me, tying it at the neck and around the back, so that my arms were confined. She led me through another set of doors. We entered the cavernous space of the theatre. She directed me towards a padded recliner chair of the kind you might find at a dentist's clinic.

There were other figures in the large room. As I sat down, one of them approached me. It was Dr Alexis. 'Hello, good morning,' he said, smiling reassuringly. I gave him an uncertain, watery smile in return. I was puzzled by the chair. How would I fall asleep sitting up?

Now two other nurses came over and draped a gauzy sheet over my head. There was a slit for my nose and mouth. The gauze meant that, even though my eyes were open, my vision was hazy. Perhaps this is why the following events were curiously dreamlike.

When Dr Alexis came forward, I barely recognized him, because he wore a cloth mask over his mouth and nose. A round mirror with a viewing aperture rode high on his forehead, held in place by black bands. Bright lights were moved into place behind me, and now, as he sat directly in front of me, he slipped the round mirror over one eye and said, 'Open mouth.' The light reflected in the mirror shone precisely into the back of my throat while he looked through the round aperture.

I thought, *Ooo! That's clever!* All this while I had been expecting to get an injection, then be asked to count to ten, falling into unconsciousness by around five. When a nurse swabbed my nose and mouth with something smelly, I thought, *That must be the anaesthetic. It'll put me to sleep. But they don't know how to tell me to count.* So I counted quietly to myself.

*One*: a nurse positioned herself behind me. *Two*: she gripped my head between her (surprisingly hard) hands. *Three*: the doctor leaned forward towards me. *Four*: EEEK! He was holding up what looked like a giant injection needle directly in front of my face! *Five*: the nurse behind me said, in heavily accented English, 'KEEP BREATHING!'

'Open mouth,' said the doctor once more.

That's when I realized there was no point counting any further. I would not be lying flat. I would not be 'asleep'. Instead, I was going to be awake throughout whatever lay ahead. It was like getting to the very top of a roller-coaster ride, seeing the horrifying plunge that I was about to take and knowing that there was nothing at all I could do about it.

I opened my mouth. What else could I have done? I was the one who had asked to be on this ride. I had to go along with it. I couldn't scream even if I wanted to, because there was a doctor sitting directly in front of me with a needle that he plunged straight into the back of my throat, directly into the red balloons. First on the left side, then on the right.

I had been going to dentists from a very young age, so I knew what a local anaesthetic was: something that caused numbness. I knew that's what the doctor was doing, and I wasn't scared of syringes. But to get injected right in the middle of the soreness in my throat, with no advance warning, no discussion, was so astonishing that I literally had no response. I didn't have time to be afraid or to think up ways of resisting.

I felt the shining tip of the needle invading the tender interior of my throat. I could even hear it as it went in, a faint crick-crick-crick followed by a phantom flood as the liquid anaesthetic was released. A moment later, a delirious numbness invaded the back of my throat. Remember it was always hurting? Suddenly, there was a total release from all sensation. First on one side, then on the other. It was as if the entire back of my throat had been turned into wood.

The next thing I knew, the doctor was reaching in with what I assumed was a scalpel, to that solid block that my throat had become. There was a flash of steel, and then he was in there, digging and gouging. I couldn't feel any kind of pain. Instead, there were other kinds of sensations that my mind could not describe in words, except as different forms of pressure. First as if the block of wood at the back of my throat was being carved, then pulled out, then cut.

The nurse behind me kept intoning, 'Keep breathing . . . Keep breathing . . .' Once or twice she tilted my head forward over a kidney dish that someone held in front of my mouth and said,

'Spit!' There was some swabbing, then some more pushing, then some prodding. My chin was given a thorough wipe.

And that was it. The surgery was over! The tonsils were gone.

Everything had happened so fast that I had absolutely no time in which to process the complete reversal of my expectations. When the gauze covering was removed, I was able to see clearly once more. I understood now what the purpose of the floor-length plastic bib was: to protect my pyjamas from the river of bright crimson blood that had spilled out of my mouth, straight down to the floor. It was the most shocking sight. I had never at any point in all my imaginings consciously thought of the blood that must inevitably accompany a surgery. I could scarcely believe that it had all come from me, because I wasn't in any pain and I hadn't felt the blood leaving me. It was like being the victim of a murder without the nuisance of having to die.

One of the nurses walked me back to my room. When my mother saw me, she jumped to her feet, saying, 'What's happened? What's happened?'

She'd assumed that I'd be wheeled back in, unconscious. The sight of me trotting in on my own two feet made her think that the operation had, for some reason, been cancelled.

I pointed to my mouth and waggled my head. 'It's OVER?' she asked, repeating herself in amazement until I said, forgetting that I mustn't talk, 'Yes. Over.'

Barely twenty minutes had passed since the time I'd left my room, but I felt dazed and turned inside out, like an umbrella in a strong gust of wind. I wasn't scared, and my throat was still completely numb. At the same time, I was no longer the same person who had light-heartedly set off early that morning, expecting to 'fall asleep'. I wasn't quite sure who I'd become.

I got another injection, in my arm this time. I'm guessing it was morphine, because I spent the rest of the day in a pleasant, drowsy cloud. When the numbness at the back of my throat finally wore off, the pain tried to return. But the morphine transformed it into a faint scratchy sensation that I could easily ignore.

Perhaps the morphine also helped me get over the tragic fate that awaited me a little later that day, at lunchtime. When the tray was brought to my room,

I saw a dish of hot grey mush with a pat of butter melting in the middle of it, an egg cup containing a raw egg (yuck!) and . . . NO ICE CREAM.

Not then, not ever, for the rest of the week. Ice cream was forbidden because of the bronchitis. I was to have the mush (sago porridge) and the egg three times a day, because they would slide down my throat painlessly. I was bitterly disappointed and, of course, absolutely refused to touch the egg, but in my newly acquired inside-out state, I could see that there was no point making a fuss. The ice-cream-less-ness was just one more surprise, along with being conscious through the surgery, the river of blood and all the rest of it. They were unpleasant surprises, but at the same time, nothing had actually gone wrong. I'd managed to get rid of my toxic, aching tonsils, and that was worth focusing on.

The rest of my week passed peacefully. I had plenty of visitors, books to read and letters to write. Sometimes a little Iraqi girl from a neighbouring room wandered in. I couldn't talk, and she didn't know any English anyway, but she liked playing with my crayons, and I was happy to share them with her.

One morning I was roused from sleep by a plump young nurse. She made the 'turn over' gesture and so I did, sleepy but curious, turning my head towards her. She raised up my pyjama top, baring my back. She had a set of small glass jars in a box, which she placed on the nightstand. Then, as I watched in amazement, she held up a pair of tongs with a large wad of cotton at the end, dipped the cotton in spirit and set it aflame! Taking each jar in turn, she lightly heated the rim and quickly stuck it down on my back.

I had absolutely no idea what was going on. The bottles didn't hurt. There was a pleasant sensation of heat and that was all. When she had placed all twelve jars, she covered me up with my blanket and made a 'stay' gesture with her hands. Naturally, that's what I did—I could hardly move around much with my back covered in glass bottles!

The lack of explanation made it seem like some crazy, meaningless ritual. For several days the skin on my back was decorated with red circles left there by the hot bottles. Years later, I would hear that this is a folk remedy called 'cupping'. It's meant to help loosen mucus in the lungs.

Eventually, I was declared fit enough to leave. I bade a tearful farewell to my nurses. When I saw Dr Alexis for the last time, he took my hands in his, looked deep into my eyes and said, '*Dasvidaniya . . . Khuda hafiz . . .* Goodbye!'

My throat healed up completely. I got masses of ice cream at home. I returned to my boarding school. Passed my exams. Did not turn into a vegetable. All is good.

When the doorbell rang and Sitaram the fruit*wala* hauled the first of the mangoes into the house, Noorie let out a sigh. *Now everyone will go all gooey-eyed as if some Shah Rukh Khan-type himself has come into the house*, she thought. *Yup, there's Mom picking up a ripe yellow mango and holding it to her nose, eyes closed in ecstasy.*

'We used to wrap these in newspaper and line them on the shelves to ripen. The whole room would be fragrant with the aroma of ripening mangoes,' Noorie's mom reminisced, her hands cradling a mango.

Dad's eyes glazed over as he backtracked into the past. 'Ras Gala—what an event that was. The whole family, all fifty of us, and the juicy *ras* of at least six different varieties of mango . . .'

'Mangoes mean summer holidays, *na?*' said Dadi, as she added a start-of-the-season tip to a beaming Sitaram's payment.

Noorie rolled her eyes. She had seen the fanatical look in Dadi's eyes and figured that almost all future meals would feature a mango in some way. Eeek! Really, there should be a law against adult nostalgia trips, particularly those that involved mangoes. What was to like about this fruit? She much preferred strawberries.

This summer hardly felt like the holidays. Noorie had a tuition calendar so packed it could rival the schedule of the busiest CEO. She picked up her maths books, reluctantly taking the piece of mango that her mom forced on her. Mom just couldn't understand that she did not like mangoes!

Out she slipped onto the landing to head downstairs, the sad piece of mango still in her palm, when the lift door opened to reveal Arushi.

Arushi of the elfin face and glossy hair. Arushi the Traitor. Arushi the Enemy from 603.

Ugh! How come she hadn't gone on summer vacation?

'So, what are you eating? Hapus, is it? Such a rubbish fruit,' Arushi sneered.

Noorie felt the blood rush to her head. Of course Arushi would find any reason to pick a fight. And of course she, Noorie, would react.

'Oh! And what kind of mango could be better than an Alphonso, the king of fruits?'

'Kesar, of course. My uncle sends us boxes of it from our farm in Gujarat.' Arushi rolled her eyes in a most annoyingly superior manner.

Noorie ignored what she decided was a crass reference to owning mango orchards and said, 'Flavourless. Simply can't compare with the Alphonso.'

'Oh yeah?' said Arushi just as the lift doors opened to the ground floor.

Without another word, both girls walked off on their respective ways. All thoughts of a peaceful holiday at an end, all Noorie could think of now was how to make Arushi eat dust. (And the Hapus mango, which she absolutely, certainly, definitely didn't care about. But Arushi needn't know that.)

That night the maid from 603 came bearing a covered tray, which she handed to Dadi. Under the cloth was a bowl of saffron-coloured aam ras. And with it was a pile of freshly fried puris. 'Nina bai sent this. The aam has just come from their farm in Gujarat.'

Dadi's eyes lit up. 'Mmm, looks great. Please say thank you to Nina.'

Noorie, who was watching her favourite show on her phone, rolled her eyes. *Show-off*, she thought. *I bet Arushi made her mom send it. Just to make me mad!*

At dinner time Noorie was even more annoyed by her family's enjoyment of the neighbourly offering. Her 'But Kesar can't compare to Hapus, na?' was met with:

'A mango is a mango.'

'And with these puris . . .'

'Come on, try it. Even you will like this.'

*Oh, you just wait, Arushi!* Noorie thought, declining all offers to try the aam ras. *I'll find some way to show you that the Alphonso is the superior mango.*

After dinner, she messaged her aunt, who was a chef, to get some ideas for dishes made from Hapus.

'The Hapus is such a perfect mango,' she said, making Noorie glow with pride, as if she had spent months growing them herself. 'It is rich and non-fibrous. Why don't you try a simple mango parfait? I'll send you the recipe.'

The next day Noorie made a grand entrance into the kitchen. And looking at her mother, who nearly dropped a pan full of veggies in shock, announced that she would be making a mango dessert. Noorie was actually cooking. What's more, she was making a *mango* dish? Double delight!

'Mango parfait? Nice! Shall we eat it for dessert this afternoon?'

'Yes. And I thought, since we can't send back empty dishes to Nina Aunty, why don't we put some of the parfait in it?' Noorie quickly turned away, trying not to laugh at her mom's stunned expression. The enmity between the two girls was legendary (even if no one knew why they were enemies).

Soon after, the maid was duly dispatched, with instructions from Mom to say that Noorie had made this specially—a piece of information that Noorie was most happy to have Arushi know.

The next day, a mango dal made by Arushi's maharaj showed up.

A mango soufflé was lobbied right back.

A quick return came in the form of a Thai mango salad.

Mom and Dadi were flummoxed by Noorie's new love for the mango, and for cooking! On the floor above, the Mehtas were equally puzzled by Arushi's similar dual obsessions.

Regardless, they did not complain. They were having a most tasty summer!

Coming back from Physics tuition, Noorie bumped into Arushi.

'Now you know? Kesar is so much better than Alphonso,' Arushi said, never one to let sleeping dogs lie.

'Oh, come on, I've given you so many examples of how superior the Hapus is. And you still keep going on about the Kesar? Typical.'

'What do you mean typical?' Arushi said belligerently.

'You never listen to what other people are saying. You only care about yourself,' Noorie said angrily.

'What?'

'It's true! When I showed you the painting that I wanted to send in for the competition, a painting I hadn't even shown my mom, you barely glanced at it.'

'Well, yeah, you have all your new school buddies to give you advice,' said Arushi with a shrug.

'Thank God for that. At least they're more supportive friends. In fact, when they came home, I was so excited for them to meet you, but you acted like such a snob.'

'You hardly talked to me when they were here. You were my best friend, and now suddenly you didn't want to hang out with me any more!'

'Not true!' yelled Noorie.

Their little shouting match had an audience of assorted wide-eyed children who came downstairs to play every day. Both girls, seething with anger, barged into the lift, each pretending that the other did not exist, which, considering that the lift was a small enclosed square of a few feet, was quite a feat!

Next day's mango jelly from Noorie enclosed a note for Arushi:

Sorry, did my friends make you feel left out?

A mango barfi came back that evening with NOT AT ALL, which left her mom really confused.

*Uff*, thought Noorie. *So stubborn.*

FINE went back a note with the mango milkshake.

You always shared everything with me. And now you just don't have time for me, said a slip of paper tucked under a dish of mango salsa.

Just because I have new friends, it didn't mean you were not my friend any more. In fact, I wanted all of us to be friends, went back a letter with some mango rasgollas.

Ha! Really? Liar. This time the note came alone. The dishes couldn't keep up with the conversation.

FINE. Yes, this note too went by itself in a mango-coloured envelope.

When they met in the lift a few days later, onlookers were disappointed by the lack of fireworks this time around.

At the annual building summer lunch Arushi and Noorie found themselves in line for the buffet. As did both their moms.

'Nina,' said Noorie's mom, 'we really enjoyed all the yummy mango dishes Arushi made.'

Arushi squirmed uncomfortably, smiling stiffly at some point in the distance.

'We also loved the goodies Noorie made. To come up with such delicious ideas she must love mangoes very much.'

Noorie shuffled her feet and looked down at her plate.

'Actually,' Noorie's mom said, 'I don't know what happened to her. Normally she hates mangoes.'

Arushi's mom looked at Noorie's. 'Really?' she said in surprise. 'You know what, so does Arushi!'

By now they had reached the dessert counters, which featured a large dish of mango pudding. Instinctively, both girls looked at each other.

'Mango?' offered Arushi.

And, although they tried hard not to, they burst out laughing. Placing a huge dollop of chocolate mousse on Arushi's plate, Noorie said, 'Never again!'

Dad's busyness failed after Jatin Uncle left. I don't like Jatin Uncle, and I'm happy he's gone. We have no money any more, Ma told us. She said Dad's company's gone bank erupt. I asked if banks are like volcanoes and she nodded, but I knew she wasn't really listening. I asked Dad if this meant we would stop going to school, but he got angry and said education came first and that he'd starve to send us to school. I don't enjoy school and Dad really enjoys eating, so his choice makes no sense. My sister loves going to school, though. I guess Dad could half-starve if he really wanted to. Then he wouldn't be so fat, too, and his dying bitties wouldn't be a problem any more. That's a disease he has. He shouldn't be eating sweets, but he does because he has a sweet tooth. When I asked him to show me his sweet tooth he said it's just a phrase.

Anyway, so we didn't go to Bali for our summer holidays like we were supposed to. Instead, we are here. In my grandparents' jungle home. I love Dada and Dadi, but Dad doesn't like them, even though they are his parents.

Dad stares out of the window all day and looks annoyed when anyone speaks to him. Outside the window is a narrow garden patch, then a river and tall trees on the other side of the river. We see bison and deer and langurs come to drink water from the river. It's so very exciting, but Dad shakes his head every time he sees any wild animal. It reminds him that his parents are crazy to live in a faraway jungle. Ma also thinks it's crazy of them but in a nice way. Ma likes crazy. She thinks Dad does too, or did till he started his busyness of making boxes with stupid Jatin Uncle, which made him uncrazy and boring.

Dada and Dadi's house is nice. It's made of logs, the floor is uneven, the walls are uneven, and there are blue, yellow and red sofas in the living room. And a green carpet. The bookshelves are red and stuffed with books, the curtains are white. The house has only two bedrooms. Nisha and I sleep in

our grandparents' large bedroom—I sleep on the bed
with them and Nisha sleeps on the sofa-cum-bed at
the other end of the room, next to the window. My
parents sleep in the small guest bedroom with a
sloping ceiling, on which Dad bumps his head when
he forgets how tall he is or how low the ceiling is
in some places. I asked him which one he forgets
but he didn't answer; he doesn't answer most of my
questions anyway.

I think Dad knows a lot of things, even though
he doesn't like answering my questions. Yesterday he
was getting bored staring out of the window, so when
I asked him if diseases make people dizzy, he gave me
a long answer about health and doctors and blood
pleasure and catatacts in Dada's eyes. But when I
asked Dada why the cat had attacked his eyes, Dad
got annoyed.

But there's one thing Dad doesn't know for sure—
the truth about Baldy Rani. That Baldy Rani is my
doll, not Nisha's. He doesn't like me to play with dolls
because of Jatin Uncle. Jatin Uncle laughed loudly
when he came home with Dad one day and saw me
taking Baldy Rani for a walk in her pram. Jatin Uncle

asked me if I was a sissy and cackled when I said no, Nisha is my sister and I am her brother.

Dad started acting like Jatin Uncle after that and always got angry when I played with my dolls. Every time. I was making fake tea for Baldy Rani in my china teapot when he got angry yesterday.

'Why are you always playing with your sister's toys?' he asked. I didn't say they were mine, even though they are.

'Let him be,' said Dadi. 'Nisha doesn't play with them anyway.'

Dad gave Dadi a dirty look and turned away to continue his favourite activity—staring out of the window and frowning.

'Do you think making tea is more fun or staring out of the window?' I asked Dadi.

'Both can be fun,' she replied. 'Depends.'

'Depends on what?' I asked, putting sugar and milk into the tea because Baldy Rani likes sugary, milky tea.

'Depends on which you like to do, of course.' Dadi said.

'Okay,' I said.

Baldy Rani is beautiful. She came from London when I was two years old. Ma had got her for Nisha, who was six years old then, but Nisha didn't really care for her. She gave her the name Baldy Rani since she has fake moulded deep-brown hair. It looks pretty even though it's fake. I loved her right away. She's a big doll, almost the same size as me when she came, but now I am much bigger than her. She is four years old, but she doesn't grow. Her neck is a little loose, so I sometimes pull it up and put food into her stomach directly. Real food like small bits of chips and sometimes even rice and chapatti. I'm hoping she'll grow a little if I give her real food, but it doesn't seem to help much. Her mouth isn't real, so I can only feed her pretend food mostly anyway.

I don't want to make tea for Baldy Rani any more, so I take her behind the house, where Dad can't see us. There are tall trees on the hill there. Dada-Dadi's jungle is in a hilly place, but it's not like there are real mountains; sometimes the road goes upwards and sometimes it doesn't and keeps going straight only.

'Like life,' said Dadi when I once asked her why the road did that. 'Sometimes up, sometimes down, sometimes at the same place forever.'

'Oh,' I said. I like Dadi and everything she says, even when I don't understand what she's saying.

Baldy Rani and I are playing catch—it's easy for me to catch her since she can't move—when Dadi comes out with her watering can.

'You've found my hiding place, Rahul,' she says. We were a little far from the house, in a cave-like sloping place that was surrounded by bushes.

'It's my hiding place too, Dadi,' I say. 'I keep dry flowers and ropes and my red car here. What do you hide? I don't see any of your things.'

'It's where I hide my fears. And then sometimes I come and stare them in the face so they get scared and go away,' Dadi explains.

'You scare your fears away? But how can you scare what scares you?' I ask.

'It's the only way,' she says. 'Or they always stay. I can show you how to do it. Not that it works every time but you can try.'

'Ok,' I say, though I don't think it will work. How can I scare away a big red door, that large, scary door that I dream about at night? Once when we went to a restaurant that had a red door, I got scared and started screaming and peed in my pants. I suppose I can be annoying. Nisha doesn't find me annoying. She says I am crazy like her.

Dadi tells me that you just have to keep looking at what you are scared of without shutting your eyes. You have to look at it hard and carefully and think about why it is scary. After some time you may find that it wasn't scary in the first place. The fear is just in your mind, not in the thing.

Dadi goes away to water her flower beds. I play with Baldy Rani for a while more. I put flowers behind her ears and put her in my red car so she can drive it. But after a while I feel bored, so I go off to look for Dadi. I could help water the flowers— I like the way the water sprouts like rain from her watering can.

When Dadi and I go into the house, the sun is already as small as an idli, and white like an idli too. Dad is in the kitchen baking cookies. He bakes awesome cookies, and this also means he is in a good mood after many, many days.

Dada locks the two doors and shuts the windows. He is singing *Jingle Bells* loudly as he goes around the house checking if we are all set for the night. That is one rule of living in a jungle house: no going out after sunset. But it is nice and cosy in the house. Though my family is crazy, I like being stuck with them like this every day. When we go back home after the holidays it'll be different. Nisha will stay in her room all the time, Ma will be busy on her laptop and Dad anyway comes home so late. Though I don't know what he will do when we go back, since his busyness is gone.

Dad brings up his busyness problems at dinner. It's boring. Nisha and I leave after a bit and go to Dada and Dadi's room. Nisha gets into bed without brushing her teeth or changing her clothes. I always brush my teeth before sleeping and change into my striped pyjamas. I go into the living room to get Baldy Rani. Dada thinks she takes up too much space on the bed and she should sleep with Nisha instead. But Nisha doesn't want her. And Baldy Rani can't fall asleep without me, because I am the only one who knows her favourite bedtime stories.

Baldy Rani isn't in the living room. I look under the sofas in case she is hiding. And on the bookshelves. I check in the two bedrooms and the small dining space and kitchen. I even check in the two bathrooms. I am beginning to panic but go all over the house once more. It's a small house and she is big, so it doesn't take long.

'Nisha, Baldy Rani isn't in the house,' I say, sinking into her bed and shaking her.

'Must be somewhere,' Nisha says after taking out her earplugs and making me repeat what I said.

'I've been searching forever,' I say.

'Oh!' says Nisha. She knows I can't go to bed without Baldy Rani. I find tears rolling down my cheeks and brush them away. I am panicked and sad. 'Weren't you out all afternoon? Was she with you?'

I am horrified. Yes, that was it. I came home with Dadi but Baldy Rani wasn't with us. I left her out there somewhere. In the jungle, where the wild things are.

'I have to go and find her,' I whisper. The idea terrifies me, but I can't leave her outside and go to sleep. My parents, however annoying they are, wouldn't do that to me or Nisha. And Baldy Rani is my offspring (it means child), as Nisha always says.

'You know you won't be allowed to,' says Nisha. She is feeling sorry for me. I can see that.

'Then I won't tell them,' I say. 'I know where Dada keeps the keys. I can open the door and go and get her before they come to bed.'

'Don't be silly,' says Nisha. 'It's not safe.'

'But I have to.' I am crying very hard now, and Nisha puts her arms around me.

'Ok, let's go,' she says, getting out of bed. Sometimes Nisha is my hero.

We creep into the hallway, where the key rack is. We can hear Dad's voice. They are still sitting around the dining table. Good. Nisha takes the big key for the main door and in one quick movement unlocks the door and pushes back the bolts. Dada oils the locks often, so the door slips open easily. We step out and swing the door shut behind us softly.

It is pitch-dark outside. Just scary black shapes and sizes everywhere. We are holding hands, and for a moment I think we should just go back and search for Baldy Rani in the morning. But I can't. I think of her terrified in the dark, and I can't.

'Do you know where you might have left her?' Nisha asks in a whisper.

'In the hiding place.' I don't want to go there but I must. The hiding place is meant to be lit up by the sun. I don't know if I want to go there in the dark.

'Where is that?' Nisha asks, and I start walking towards it, that cave-like slippery sloping place, almost like a room in the middle of the jungle. I can see it in the distance but it looks different in the dark. As if there is a door in front of the cave. The door of my dreams. The scary large red door to a closed room.

I stumble in the dark. I don't want to go on. Nisha's hand is in mine and she's moving forward.

The door is growing. It looks exactly like it does in my dreams. Big, thick, red wood but slightly transparent, so I can see inside even though the door is closed. We are right in front of the door now. I lift my hand and point.

'Inside there?' asks Nisha. 'Let's go?'

But I am stuck. The door is still red and wooden, but it's getting more transparent by the minute. Inside is a room, a long steel room, big and square with no windows, like the inside of a cave. And inside the room is my bed. Nothing else. Just my bed. And a man sitting on it. A man in a suit and tie, sitting up straight and smiling at me. It's Jatin Uncle, and he's got Baldy Rani on his lap. I start screaming and then I put my hand over my mouth so the screams are inside me now, going around and around in my stomach and chest. It's exactly how it happens in my dreams.

Nisha is kneeling in front of me. Her face is grey in the dark, and she looks so worried. I stop screaming. I look at my sister. I love my sister. And I love Baldy Rani. I have to go into the cave, into that room, and get her from Jatin Uncle. I have to save her.

We go into the cave, hand in hand, but I am still terrified. My eyes are half-shut because I am so scared, but I can see the steel walls and floor and cot. Nisha squeezes my hand and I force myself to open my eyes fully, because I remember Dadi saying in the morning that looking at it properly will make the scary thing go away. I look straight at the door and my bed. I remember the evening I entered my bedroom and found Jatin Uncle sitting on my bed. I pushed open the door to my room and got so surprised to find him sitting on my bed and holding Baldy Rani. He told me how silly and weak I was, like a girl, a sissy. He kept talking, sitting up straight and smiling all while saying those mean things.

The door to my room wasn't even shut that day. I could have just left, but I didn't. I couldn't even move while Jatin Uncle kept saying those mean things. I couldn't turn, I was stuck, and that night I had the scary-red-door dream for the first time. I dreamt of a red door behind which I knew Jatin Uncle was waiting for me in a steel room, holding Baldy Rani in one hand and laughing at me. I have that dream very often, almost every night.

And just like that, I know Dadi is right. I remember the scary door and I think about it carefully, and the door isn't scary at all. How can a door be scary? It's what's behind the door that's scary. That thing with Jatin Uncle did happen, but it's not going to happen again, because Jatin Uncle has gone away now. Suddenly I find Jatin Uncle is not sitting behind the door any more. He's gone away. Ma had promised I would never again have to meet him. Because he was mean and bad. Baldy Rani is lying on the ground, the floor of the cave—it's not the steel room any more. Nisha picks her up and gives her to me. I hold Baldy Rani tight and hug her close. As we go out of the cave, I look back and the cot is gone, and the steel walls too. It's just my hiding place again. I have scared away what I was scared of. I have done it. Jatin Uncle is only a stupid old man. And I will never have to see him again. Ma did pinky promise, so that means I really never will.

We slip into the house. Just in time. They are getting up from the table now. Nisha locks and bolts the door and runs to put the key back on the key rack. Then we are in bed as if we never left it. Baldy Rani is cold and smells of jungle. I don't know how I could forget her like that. But, as Ma says, even parents make mistakes. And I am only six years old. I am happy when Dadi gets into the bed and puts her arm around me.

'I scared away what I am scared of, Dadi,' I say.

'Good. I knew you could do it,' says Dadi. 'I'm proud of you.'

I am proud of me too. I wish we could live in Dada-Dadi's jungle home forever. School sucks. But never mind. I know I won't dream of that door again. And what lies behind it. Doors are just doors.

I feel happy as I hug Baldy Rani while Dadi hugs me.

Today Ajja, Ajji and Vishnu Kaka were all feeling sad. The children's holidays were nearly over, and it was nearing the time when they would go back to their homes. For three weeks the houses had echoed with their laughter, games and quarrels. Now all would be quiet once again, till they returned for the next holiday.

The children too were feeling sad, and had gathered around their grandparents in a tight little group.

Raghu, the eldest, said, 'We had more fun this holiday then we've ever had. Even more than when we visited Disneyland. And it was all because of the stories.'

Ajja said, 'When I was still working as a schoolteacher, I always found it was so much easier to get my students' attention when I told the lessons in the form of stories.'

Anand said, 'I find it really boring to read history from a book. But if you tell us the stories from history, I'm sure we will remember everything!' Everyone now trained their bright eyes on Ajji.

'How can you tell us only one story even on this last day, Ajji! We want more!' they clamoured.

But Ajji shook her head. 'If you eat only pickles and laddoos, will you be healthy? Stories are like that. You can't spend all your time listening to stories. Then it will be boring. Like the unending story that a king once had to hear.'

'I want a story! And that's an order!' shouted King Pratap Singh of Mayanagar. King Pratap was only fifteen years old, and still a boy at heart. He didn't like being a king much, because he was supposed to be doing serious things like keeping the law, listening to his people's problems and all kinds of dreary things like that. The only part he liked about being a ruler was that everyone had to obey him! How he loved giving orders and making all kinds of demands. And what he loved the most was listening to stories! Every day, he insisted on listening to at least ten stories. All the storytellers in his kingdom lined up at his court. They told him funny stories, scary stories, magical stories and anything else that came to their minds. King Pratap listened to all with rapt attention.

He loved stories and storytellers so much that whenever he heard a good tale he would shower the teller with gold, silver and all kinds of wonderful presents. His ministers sighed and shook their heads and tried to explain, 'Your Majesty, stories are all very well, but you should be listening to them after your work is done! Your people need you to do so many things for them. If you spend all your time wrapped up in fantasies, how will the land prosper?'

But King Pratap paid no attention. It was stories he wanted, and stories he would get. But how long could the people provide him with stories? Soon the tales began to dry up. Some tried to cleverly tell him ones they had related long back, but Pratap was sharp as a needle. 'I've heard that one! Off with his head for repeating a story!'

Oh, how his ministers had to plead with him to pardon the culprits!

Finally, disgusted with all the storytellers in his land, the king announced, 'I want someone to tell me a story that will go on and on, till I ask him to stop. Anyone who can do this will get half my kingdom as a prize!'

His ministers were even more horrified at this. Half the kingdom to some woolly-headed writer and teller of stories! How horrible! They all tried to show the king the foolishness of his ways, but he was adamant.

A story that lasted for days, even weeks, was what he wanted, and that was that!

Soon a long line of men and women appeared at his court. Each one wanted to win the big prize. But none of their stories were good enough for King Pratap.

'Boring!' he shouted at some.

'Rubbish!' he yelled at others.

'Cock and bull!' he bellowed at yet others.

Meanwhile, work on the kingdom's affairs had come to a stop. All the ministers were sitting wringing their hands and wondering how to bring back their king to solving all the important issues. Finally, the chief minister, who was wise and clever, had an idea.

The next day, a scruffy, crazy-looking man turned up at the court. His hair was a mess, his clothes were half-torn and on his feet he wore torn shoes from which his toes stuck out. He marched up to the palace and demanded to be given an audience with the king. The guards sighed and let him in. They were used to having all kinds of characters turning up at the gates wanting to tell stories to the king.

The old man was admitted into the king's chamber. There he made himself comfortable, drank a huge jug of water and, without introducing himself, started his story:

'This story begins in a humble farmer's field. The farmer had toiled days and weeks and months and grown a bumper crop of sugar cane. He sold the sugar cane to the nearby sugar factory and they made sacks and sacks of sugar out of it. Everyone was so happy. All this sugar would be sold in the markets and make everyone very rich! That year their children would get nice new clothes, their stores would be full of food and their wives would be very happy with them!

'Now all that sugar had to be stored and kept carefully till the sacks could be taken to the market to sell. The factory people poured the sugar into many sacks and lugged them into a storeroom. In the storeroom who would you find but a colony of ants. They had decided that building their house near such a ready supply of their favourite food was a very good idea, and were always on the lookout for new batches of sugar to be stored there.

'No sooner had the sacks been kept than the lines of ants marched up to them. They found little holes to make their way in and the first ant went into the first bag of sugar, took one sugar crystal and went back.

'The next ant went into the bag and took a crystal and returned home.

'Another went into the bag and took a crystal and returned home.

'Yet another went into the bag and took a crystal and returned home . . .'

So on and on the storyteller droned. King Pratap found he had nearly dozed off, the day had passed and he was still listening to the same story.

'Stop! Stop!' he ordered. 'I will listen to the rest of the story tomorrow.'

The next morning the old man turned up as usual and started from where he had left off the previous day.

'Yesterday I was telling you how the ants came and picked up the sugar crystals. Now the next ant went towards the bag of sugar and took a crystal and went back home. Another went and took a sugar crystal and returned home. Another ant . . .'

The story went on and on like this. Lunch and dinner passed, but nothing new happened. By now King Pratap was bursting with rage. How dare anyone tell him such a boring story? 'What kind of a story is this?' he complained. 'What will happen next? What happened to the farmer?'

But the old man only smiled and said, 'Have patience, Your Majesty. That year the yield was very good, and there were thousands of bags of sugar. I have to tell you how the ants collected all the sugar.'

'Oh, stop! Stop!' Pratap shouted. 'Stop this boring story at once!'

The man now stood up and said, 'Fine. If you are ordering me to stop, I have won the prize. Give me half your kingdom!'

The king was in a dilemma now. He had announced a competition and prize no doubt, but could he honestly give away half the kingdom to this crazy-looking storyteller with his boring tale? As he sat pondering, the man grinned even wider and took off his dirty robe, rubbed off the dirt from his face and shook back his shaggy white hair. Everyone was astonished. Why, this was the chief minister himself!

'Don't worry, Your Majesty,' the minister told his overjoyed king. 'I did not want half your kingdom. I only wanted to show you how you were wrong to neglect your work and listen to stories night and day. Your people deserve a good king, someone who will work hard to look after them; someone who will think of his own happiness only once his people are happy. That's what good kings do, you know, not just give orders and enjoy yourself.'

Poor Pratap looked ashamed at this. Yes, he had been an extremely selfish king. From now on, story time would only be at night, after all his work was done.

So that was how the summer holidays ended. Everyone packed their bags and reached the station. Their mothers had come to take them back home. Ajja, Ajji, Vishnu Kaka, Damu, Rehmat Chacha—everyone had come to see them off. No one felt like leaving Ajji's side, and Meenu kept hugging her till she had to board the train.

Soon the train puffed out of the station. The children leaned out to wave their goodbyes. Slowly Shiggaon got left behind. But the children would continue to remember their Ajja and Ajji and everyone else, and all the stories, which would remain with them forever. And they would be back, during the next summer holidays, when they would hear so many more . . .

A version of this story first appeared in *Grandma's Bag of Stories*.

# NOTES ON THE AUTHORS

**Nayanika Mahtani** is the author of *Ambushed* and *The Gory Story of Genghis Khan (a.k.a. Don't Mess with the Mongols)*. She lives in London with her family and their two goldfish named Sushi and Fishfinger.

**Paro Anand** can't stop writing, and has written for children and young people for over thirty years. She has published twenty-six books, including novels, short-story collections, plays, picture books, a teacher's guide and, most recently, a graphic novel.

**Jane De Suza** is the writer of the popular SuperZero series, books for adults and kids, stories, app and game designs and a column for the *Hindu*. She lives in Singapore with three guys (related to her) and two visiting mynahs (who aren't).

**Ruskin Bond** has written over 500 short stories, essays and novellas, and more than forty books for children. He received the Sahitya Akademi Award in 1992, the Padma Shri in 1999 and the Padma Bhushan in 2014.

**Shabnam Minwalla** is a mother of three. In the little off-time that this brain-scrambling job permits, she writes articles for magazines and newspapers, and popular books for children. Her eight books include *What Maya Saw* and *The Six Spellmakers of Dorabji Street*.

**Subhadra Sen Gupta** has written over forty books for children because she thinks they are the best readers in the world. She writes on history; imagines mystery, ghost and adventure stories; and dreams up comic books.

**Khyrunnisa A.**, prize-winning author of children's fiction, loves reading, writing and children. She created the popular comic character Butterfingers for the children's magazine *Tinkle*. Her latest book is called *Of Course It's Butterfingers!*.

**Nandini Nayar** has written more than forty books for children. These include picture books, novels, adaptations, fictional biographies and retellings. For more information about her, go to www.nandininayar.in.

**Prashant Pinge** resides in sixteenth-century England, next to the Bard's house, where he spends his days in the company of his characters and his nights taming wild dragons. He does surface from time to time to update his website, www.prashantpinge.com.

**Rabindranath Tagore** was a pioneering literary figure, renowned for his ceaseless innovations in poetry, prose, drama, music and painting, which he took up late in life. In 1913 he was awarded the Nobel Prize for Literature. His story *A Feast for Rats*, excerpted from *The Land of Cards: Stories, Poems and Plays for*

*Children*, is translated by eminent writer, critic and translator **Radha Chakravarty**.

**Manjula Padmanabhan** is an author, playwright and cartoonist. Her books include *Getting There*, a quirky travel memoir; *Harvest*, winner of the 1997 Onassis Prize for Theatre; *Escape*, a dark adventure novel; and two collections featuring her fuzzy-haired comic-strip character, Suki.

Former journalist **Lubaina Bandukwala** became a children's writer and editor for a simple reason: now she can read as many children's books as she likes and call it grown-up work! And because guilty pleasures must be shared, she founded her own children's literature festival—Peek A Book.

**Himanjali Sankar** is a writer and editor who loves dogs, oceans and blue nail polish. She doesn't like face powder and people who shout at her. Her latest book is called *The Lies We Tell*.

**Sudha Murty** is a social activist, popular author and chairperson of the Infosys Foundation. A prolific writer in English and Kannada, she has written novels, technical books, travelogues, collections of short stories and non-fiction pieces, and seven bestselling books for children.